LET'S STUDY KOREAN :
Complete Practice Work Book for Grammar, Spelling, Vocabulary
and Reading Comprehension With Over 600 Questions

ISBN 979-11-88195-34-3

BRIDGE EDUCATION

Ordering Information:
Quantity sales. Special discounts are available on quantity
purchases by corporations, associations, and others.
For details, contact the publisher at the email address above.

Printed in the United States of America

www.newampersand.com
14 13 12 11 10 / 10 9 8 7 6 5 4 3 2 1

Table of Contents

The following words are incomplete.

Insert correct consonants, vowels, and batchim.

Hak Gyo : School

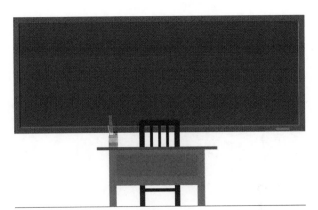

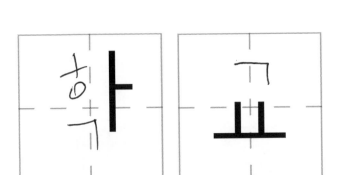

Bu Mo Nim : Parents

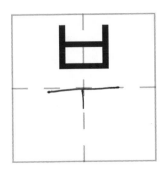 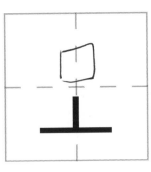 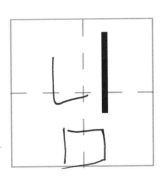

Gang Ah Ji : Puppy

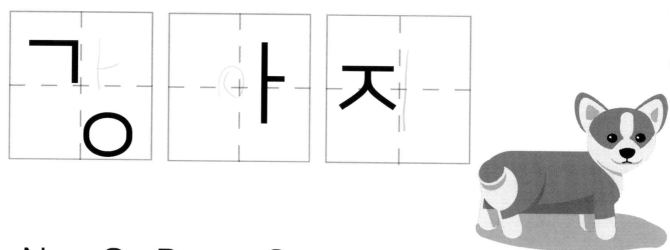

Nun Sa Ram : Snowman

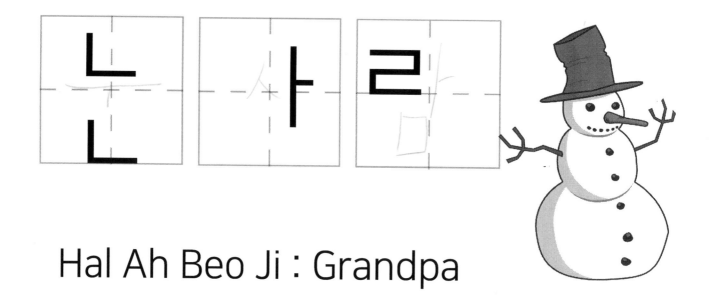

Hal Ah Beo Ji : Grandpa

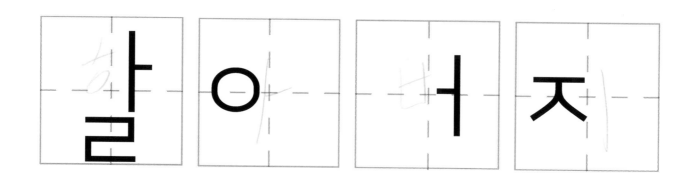

In a similar fashion, 은/는 serve as a topic marking particle. They are also added to the end of the subject a sentence, followed by a predicate, and designate the main idea or topic.

'은' is used for words ending in a consonant (i.e., with 받침), while '는' is used for words ending in a vowel (i.e., without 받침). Try filling in the boxes.

저 은 학생입니다.	귀신 은 무서워요.
수박 은 맛있다.	당신 은 몇 살 이세요?

On the other hand, 을/를 serves as an object marking particle. They are added to the end of a subject to mark the object of the sentence, and . As the name suggests, they are followed by an action verb.

'을' is used for words ending in a consonant (i.e., with 받침), while '를' is used for words ending in a vowel (i.e., without 받침). Try filling in the boxes.

지갑 ☐ 잃어버렸다.	책 ☐ 읽어요.
눈사람 ☐ 만들어요.	편지 ☐ 씁니다.

Number the following pieces in the correct order to complete a sentence.

I study Korean.

□	□	□	□
나는	한다.	한국어	공부를

I am going to have (eat) dinner with my parents.

□	□	□	□
부모님과	저녁을	갑니다	먹으러

Cheol Soo comes back from school at 3:00 PM.

□	□	□	□
돌아온다.	오후 3시에	학교에서	철수는

Let's study Korean very hard.

□	□	□
한국어를	공부하자.	열심히

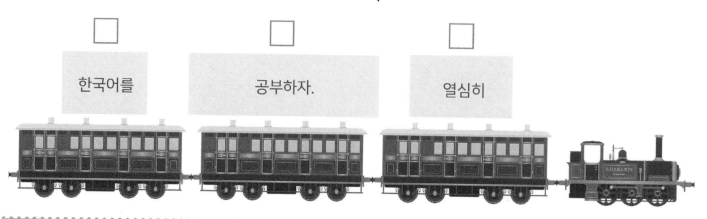

Answer Key

1 - 4 - 2 - 3   /   1 - 2 - 4 - 3   /   4 - 3 - 2 - 1   /   1 - 3 - 2

Connect the correct particles with the subject.

송아지 [calf] ●

수박 [watermelon] ●   ● 이

하늘 [sky] ●

책 [book] ●   ● 가

철수 [cheol-su] ●

내 친구 [my friend] ●   ● 은

책상 [desk] ●

컴퓨터 [computer] ●   ● 는

자동차 [car] ●

침대 [bed] ●   ● 을

방석 [cushion] ●

가방 [bag] ●   ● 를

Answer Key

송아지가.　수박이.　하늘이.　책이.
철수는.　내 친구는.　책상은.　컴퓨터는.
자동차를.　침대를.　방석을.　가방을.

Circle the 주어 to make a sentence.

얼굴에	빨리	배가	고프다.
갑니다.	다리가	천천히	아프다.
회사에	기차가	왜	떠났다.
커피가	완전히	한번	뜨겁다.

Circle the right particle.

호랑이
tiger

가   이

나비
butterfly

가   이

수박
watermelon

은   는

강아지
puppy

은   는

태양
sun

은   는

노래
song

을   를

영화
movie

을   를

왕관
crown

을   를

Some of the particles in the following sentences are used incorrectly. Read carefully and find <u>ONLY</u> those that are used incorrectly and write them down underneath it.

로보트을 만들었어요. 공부를 많이 했어요.
I made a robot.   I studied a lot.

___

맥주이 맛있다. 소금는 짜다. 하늘이 맑다.
Beer tastes good.   Salt is salty.   Sky is clear.

___

노래를 불러요. 스포츠카은 빠르다. 하마는 입가 크다.
Sing a song.   Sports cars are fast.   Hippos have a big mouth.

___

공부가 즐겁다. 책읽기는 재밌다. 영어은 어려워요.
Studying is enjoyable.   Reading is fun.   English is difficult.

___

피자는 맛있다. 고추은 매워요. 호랑이가 달려간다. I
Pizza is tasty.   Chili is hot.   Tiger is running.

___

원숭이은 귀엽다. 치타는 빠르다. 전화를 받습니다.
Monkeys are cute.   Cheetas are fast.   I answer the phone.

___

음악을 듣습니다. 영화을 봅니다. 라면를 먹습니다.
I listen to music.   I watch a movie.   I eat ramyeon.

___

Answer Key

로보트를 만들었어요. 맥주가 맛있다. 소금은 짜다. 스포츠카는 빠르다. 하마는 입이 크다. 영어는 어려워요. 고추는 매워요. 원숭이는 귀엽다. 영화를 봅니다. 라면을 먹습니다.

SUBJECT / OBJECT / PARTICLES
주어 / 목적어 / 조사

Question 1 - 20. Identify the SUBJECT (주어) of the sentences. If there are more than one, choose the one that have both.

1. 하늘이 맑다. (The sky is clear.)

A.늘 B.늘이 C.하늘 D.이 E.맑다

2. 장미가 예쁘다. (The rose is pretty.)

A.장 B.미가 C.가 D.장미 E.예쁘

3. 음식이 맛있다. (The food is delicious.)

A.음식이 B.맛있 C.맛 D.음식 E.있

4. 갑자기 바람이 분다. (Wind blew suddenly.)

A.갑 B.갑자 C.바람 D.분 E.분다

5. 모자가 매우 작다. (The hat is very small.)

A.매우 B.작다 C.모자 D.모자 / 매우 E.모자 / 작다

6. 예쁜 강아지가 뛰어가고 있습니다. (A pretty puppy is running away.)

A.예쁜 B.뛰어 C.강아지 D.강아지 / 뛰어 E.있습니다

7. 나비가 날아와 꽃에 앉았다. (A butterfly flew in and sat on a flower.)

A.날아와 B.나비 C.날아 D.꽃에 E.앉았다

8. 제 이름은 김철수입니다. (My name is Kim Cheol-soo.)

A.김철수 B.제 C.김철수 / 제 D.김철수 / 이름 E.이름

9. 시원한 바람이 불었다. (Cool wind blew.)

A.시원 B.시원한 C.불면 D.좋겠다 E.바람

10. 어두운 구름이 빠르게 없어지고 있습니다. (Dark cloud is disappearing fast.)

A.어두운 B.구름 C.빠르게 D.없어지고 E.있습니다

11. 지갑을 잃어버린 철수가 슬퍼하고 있습니다. (Cheol-soo, lost his wallet, is feeling sad.)

A.지갑 B.철수 C.슬퍼 D.잃어버린 E.지갑 / 철수

12. 영희와 철수가 눈사람을 만들고 있습니다. (Yeong-hi and Cheol-soo are making a snowman.)

A.눈사람 B.영희 / 철수 C.만들고 D.영희 / 철수 / 눈사람 E.희와

13. 철수가 영희를 보고 웃었다. (Cheol-soo smiled at Yeong-hi.)

A.철수 B.영희 C.철수 / 영희 D.철수가 영희 E.웃었다.

14. 민수는 무서운 영화를 보면 악몽을 꾼다.
(Min-soo has a nightmare when he watches a scary movie.)

A.민수 B.무서운 / 보면 C.영화 / 악몽 D.꾼다 E.영화를

15. 한라산은 얼마나 높을까? (I wonder how high Mt. Halla is?)

A.한라산 B.높 C.얼마나 D.한라산 / 높을 E.한라산 / 높을까

16. 사나운 사자가 뛰어가고 있습니다. (A fierce lion is running around.)

A.사나운 B.사자 C.사자가 D.뛰어 E.있습니다

17. 사과는 건강에 아주 좋습니다. (Apple is very good for health.)

A.사과 B.사과 / 건강 C.아주 D.사과 / 아주 E.좋습니다.

18. 고기는 단백질을 많이 함유하고 있다. (Meat contains a lot of protein.)

A.고기 B.단백질 C.함유 D.고기 / 단백질 E.고기 / 함유

19. 학생은 공부를 열심히 해야 한다. (A student must study hard.)

A.학생은 B.학생 C.공부 D.열심히 E.학생 / 공부

20. 따뜻한 수프는 감기를 빨리 낫게 해준다. (Warm soup helps recover from a cold.)

A.따뜻한 B.수프 C.따뜻한 수프 D.감기 E.해준다

Question 21 - 40. Choose the correct OBJECT MARKING PARTICLE 을/를 to complete the sentence.

21. 사과( ) 먹는다. (I/she/he eat(s) an apple.)

A.을 B.를

22. 제 이름( ) 아세요? (Do you know my name?)

A.을 B.를

23. 하늘( ) 보면 마음이 상쾌해진다. (I feel refreshed when I look at the sky.)

A.을 B.를

24. 전화기( ) 꺼주세요. (Please turn off your phone.)

A.을 B.를

25. 저녁 식사로 짜장면( ) 먹어야겠다! (I shall have jja-jang-myeon for dinner!)

A.을 B.를

26. 내가 하는 말( ) 잘 들어라. (Listen carefully to what I say.)

A.을 B.를

27. 엄마( ) 보면 나랑 많이 닮은 것 같지 않니?
(Doesn't my mom look like me a lot when you look at her?)

A.을 B.를

28. 닭( ) 보면 공룡이 생각나지 않니?
(Don't chickens remind you of dinosaurs when you look at them?)

A.을 B.를

29. 소금( ) 많이 먹으면 짜요. (It's salty when you eat it too much.)

A.을 B.를

30. 축구( ) 할까? (Shall we play soccer?)

A.을 B.를

31. 야구( ) 할까, 농구( ) 할까? (Shall we play baseball or basketball?)

A.을 / 을 B.를 / 를 C. 을 / 를 D. 를 / 을

32. 닭고기( ) 먹을까, 돼지고기( ) 먹을까? (Shall we eat chicken or pork?)

A.을 / 을 B.를 / 를 C. 을 / 를 D. 를 / 을

33. 나( ) 보면, 누구( ) 떠올리니? (Who do I remind you of?)

A.을 / 을 B.를 / 를 C. 을 / 를 D. 를 / 을

34. 달콤한 사탕( ) 좋아하니, 새콤한 레몬( ) 좋아하니?
(Do you like sweet candies or sour lemons?)

A.을 / 을 B.를 / 를 C. 을 / 를 D. 를 / 을

35. 물( ) 너무 많이 마시면 건강( ) 해칠 수 있다.
(Drinking too much water can damage your health.)

A.을 / 을 B.를 / 를 C. 을 / 를 D. 를 / 을

36. 햄버거에 치즈( ) 두 장 넣고, 빵( ) 얹으세요.
(Put two slices of cheese and put on a bread.)

A.을 / 을 B.를 / 를 C. 을 / 를 D. 를 / 을

37. 바지( ) 입고, 자켓( ) 입으세요. (Put on the pants and put on a jacket.)

A.을 / 을 B.를 / 를 C. 을 / 를 D. 를 / 을

38. 피망( ) 좋아하니, 양파( ) 좋아하니? (Do you like bell peppers or onions?)

A.을 / 을 B.를 / 를 C. 을 / 를 D. 를 / 을

39. 고개( ) 높이 들고 저 앞( ) 똑바로 보아라. (Lift your chin up and look straight in front.)

A.을 / 을 B.를 / 를 C. 을 / 를 D. 를 / 을

40. 여행( ) 가면 사진( ) 많이 찍어야지! (I shall take a lot of pictures when I travel!)

A.을 / 을 B.를 / 를 C. 을 / 를 D. 를 / 을

Question 41 - 60. Choose the correct SUBJECT MARKING PARTICLE 이/가 **to complete the sentence.**

41. 비행기( ) 도착했다. (The plane has arrived.)

A.이 B.가

42. 당신 이름( ) 뭐였죠? (What was your name?)

A.이 B.가

43. 하늘( ) 맑으면 마음이 상쾌해진다. (If the sky is clear, my mind get becomes refresehd.)

A.이 B.가

44. 사과( ) 정말 달다! (Apple is really sweet!)

A.이 B.가

45. 내일 비( ) 안오면 좋겠다! (I wish it doesn't rain tomorrow!)

A.이 B.가

46. 무서운 괴물( ) 크게 소리쳤다. (Scary monster yelled loudly.)

A.이 B.가

47. 엄마( ) 만들어주신 맛있는 불고기 요리. (Tasty dish of bulgogi which my mom made me.)

A.이 B.가

48. 철수( ) 중학생이 되었다고 ? (Cheol-soo became a middle school student?)

A.이 B.가

49. 소금(　) 많이 뿌려져서 짜요. (It's salty because a lot of salt has been sprinkled.)

A.이　B.가

50. 게임(　) 그렇게 재밌어? (Is the game that much fun?)

A.이　B.가

51. 야구(　) 좋아, 농구(　) 좋아? (Do you like baseball or basketball?)

A.이 / 이　B.가 / 가　C. 이 / 가　D. 가 / 이

52. 닭(　) 먼저일까, 달걀(　) 먼저일까? (Is chicken first or egg first?)

A.이 / 이　B.가 / 가　C. 이 / 가　D. 가 / 이

53. 제(　) 말한 다음에 여러분(　) 따라하세요. (After I speak, you repeat.)

A.이 / 이　B.가 / 가　C. 이 / 가　D. 가 / 이

54. 생선 구이(　) 좋아, 비빔밥(　) 좋아? (Do you like grilled fish or bibimbap?)

A.이 / 이　B.가 / 가　C. 이 / 가　D. 가 / 이

55. 내일 아침(　) 되면, 편지(　) 도착하겠지!
(The letter should arrive when it becomes tomorrow morning!)

A.이 / 이　B.가 / 가　C. 이 / 가　D. 가 / 이

56. 햄버거에 치즈(　) 없어서, 맛(　) 없네요.
 (It's not tasty because there's no cheese in hamburger.)

A.이 / 이　B.가 / 가　C. 이 / 가　D. 가 / 이

57. TV 리모컨(　) 없어져서, 아빠(　) 화나셨다.
(Dad got upset because the TV remote has gone missing.)

A.이 / 이　B.가 / 가　C. 이 / 가　D. 가 / 이

58. 택시( ) 너무 느리게 가서, 손님( ) 소리를 질렀다.
(Customer yelled because the taxi was going too slowly.)

A.이 / 이   B.가 / 가   C. 이 / 가   D. 가 / 이

59. 산에 불( ) 나서 소방 헬기( ) 출동했다.
(A helicopter was dispatched because there was a fire on the mountain.)

A.이 / 이   B.가 / 가   C. 이 / 가   D. 가 / 이

60. 컴퓨터( ) 고장나서 전원( ) 켜지지가 않아!
(Computer broke and power won't turn on!)

A.이 / 이   B.가 / 가   C. 이 / 가   D. 가 / 이

Question 61 - 80. fill in the blank using a correct particle PARTICLE 을/를, 은/는, 이/가 to complete the sentence.

61. 나( ) 너( ) 정말로 사랑해. (I really love you.)

62. 닭고기( ) 치즈보다, 지방( ) 적다. (Chicken has less fat than cheese.)

63. 야구( ) 보다가, 재미가 없어서 영화( ) 보았다.
(I was watching baseball, but watched a movie because it was boring.)

64. 김치( ) 맵지만, 유산균( ) 많아서 건강에 좋다.
(Kimchi is spicy but it's good for health because there are a lot of probiotics.)

65. 세상에( ) 정말로 많은 나라들( ) 있구나.
(There are really many countries in the world.)

66. 차( ) 많이 막혀서 친구( ) 만나지 못했다.
(I couldn't meet my friend because there was too much traffic.)

67. 자동차( ) 10,000개의 부품( ) 사용해 만들어진다.
(Cars are made using 10,000 parts.)

68. 철수( ) 라면( ) 먹을때 항상 우유( ) 마신다.
(Cheol-soo always drinks milk when he eats ramyeon.)

69. 외국인들( ) 한국의 여름( ) 가장 좋다고 말한다.
(Foreigners say they like Summer of Korea the best.)

70. 빵( ) 먹을때는 음료수( ) 같이 마셔야지!
(You should drink a beverage when you are eating bread!)

71. 민구( ) 게임( ) 하면 시간( ) 가는 줄 모른다.
(Mingu loses track of time when he plays games.)

72. 하늘( ) 바라보니, 태양( ) 너무 강렬해서 눈( ) 감았다.
(When looking at the sky, the sun was too strong that I closed the eyes.)

73. 목욕( ) 하니까 피로( ) 풀린 철수( ) 금세 잠들었다.
(Cheol-soo fell asleep immediately after a bath because it made him feel relaxed.)

74. 선생님( ) 말하셨다. "철수( ) 일어나서 큰 소리로 책( ) 읽어라."
(Teacher said, "Cheol-soo, stand up and read the book out aloud")

75. 내일( ) 토요일. 그러면 내일 모레( ) 일요일이니까, 교회에 가서 예배( ) 드려야겠다.
(Tomorrow is Saturday, then the day after tomorrow is Sunday. I should go to church.)

76. 나( ) 너무 배가 불러서 디저트( ) 하나도 먹지 못해서 기분( ) 좋지 않았다.
(I couldn't eat any dessert because I was too full, and it made me feel upset.)

77. 공부( ) 하나도 못해서 시험 성적( ) 엉망이다.
(Test scores are a mess because I couldn't study at all.)

78. 내( ) 입양한 강아지( ) 몸( ) 아파서 약( ) 먹였는데, 열( ) 낮아지지 않았다.
(The dog I adopted was sick and I gave it a medicine, but the fever didn't get any lower.)

79. 고양이( ) 자신의 영역( ) 지키기 위해서 사람( ) 공격할 수 있다.
(Cats might attack people in order to protect their territory.)

80. 영화( ) 보고 싶었는데, 같이 보기로 한 친구( ) 시간( ) 없어서 나 혼자 보았다.
(I wanted to see a movie, but the friend who was supposed to go with me didn't have time, so I saw it alone.)

Question 81 - 100. Find to see IF the particles are used incorrectly and write the correct ones underneath them.

81. 로보트을 만들었어요.
(I made a robot.)

82. 철수은 책을 읽다가 힘이 들어서 산책를 하러 공원에 나갔습니다.
(Cheol-soo felt tired while reading a book, so he went to the park for a stroll.)

83. 스마트폰는 우리의 생활를 바꾸어 놓은 테크놀로지다.
(Smartphones are a technology that changed our life.)

84. 맥주을 마시면 배가 부르지만 기분가 좋아진다.
(Drinking beer makes me full but makes me feel good.)

85. 피자는 어린이들만 좋아하는 음식가 아니라, 어른들도 좋아한다.
(Pizza is liked not only by children but also by adults.)

86. 원숭이의 바나나을 좋아한다는 이야기는 사실이었어!
(It was true that monkeys like bananas!)

87. 안경를 잃어버린 철수는 앞가 잘 보이지 않아서 고생했다.
(Cheol-soo, who list his glasses, had a hard time.)

88. 문장의 의미을 모르면 뜻를 이해하는 게 쉽지 않다.
(If you don't know the meaning of a sentence, it's difficult to understand it.)

89. 코끼리의 옆에 있으면, 사람의 정말 작아 보인다. 반대로, 강아지가 옆에 있으면, 사람가 커 보인다. (If a man stands next to an elephant, he looks really small. Conversely, if a man stands next to a puppy, he looks big.)

90. 엄마가 아빠에게 문자을 보냈다. "집에 올때 마트에서 고기을 사오세요."
(Mom sent dad a text. "Buy meat from the mart on your way home.")

91. 한국의 여름는 너무 더워서 노인들이 힘들어한다.
(Korean summer is too hot and senior citizens have a difficult time."

92. 기분가 좋지 않으면 노래를 크게 불러보자!
(Let's sing a song aloud if you don't feel down!)

93. 술를 너무 많이 마시면 건강가 나빠진다!
(If you drink too much alcohol, your health will be damaged!")

94. 공부을 열심히 하면, 너의 꿈가 이루어 질 거야.
(If you study hard, your dream will be realized.)

95. 잠를 안자고 스마트폰을 가지고 놀면, 피곤해진다.
(If you keep playing with smart phone and not sleep, you will be tired.)

96. 소나무에 솔방울가 크게 열렸다. 사다리를 가지고 와서 따볼까?
(A pine tree has a large pine cone. Shall we bring a ladder and pick them?)

97. 운동를 너무 열심히 했더니 몸가 피곤하구나.
(I feel tired because I worked out too hard.)

98. 연습를 많이 해야 실력의 좋아지지.
(You should practice a lot to get better skills.)

99. 한글를 공부하면, 한국어 실력의 훨씬 좋아질 거야!
(If you study Hangul, your Korean skills will be much better!)

100. 나보다 나이가 많은 사람를 만나면, 예의을 갖춰서 말해야 한다.
(If I meet someone who's older than me, I should talk formally.)

Answer Key

1. C		56. D	
2. D		57. C	
3. D		58. D	
4. C		59. C	
5. C		60. D	

1. C
2. D
3. D
4. C
5. C
6. C
7. B
8. A
9. E
10. B
11. B
12. B
13. A
14. A
15. A
16. B
17. A
18. A
19. B
20. B
21. B
22. A
23. A
24. B
25. A
26. A
27. B
28. A
29. A
30. B
31. B
32. B
33. B
34. A
35. A
36. D
37. D
38. C
39. D
40. A
41. B
42. A
43. A
44. B
45. B
46. A
47. B
48. B
49. A
50. A
51. B
52. A
53. D
54. D
55. C

56. D
57. C
58. D
59. C
60. D
61. 는/를
62. 가/이
63. 를/를
64. 는/이
65. 는/이
66. 가/를
67. 는/을
68. 가/을/를
69. 은/이
70. 을/를
71. 는/을/이
72. 을/이/을
73. 을/가/가
74. 이/야/을
75. 은/는/를
76. 는/를/이
77. 를/이
78. 가/가/이/을/이
79. 는/을/을
80. 를/가/이
81. 로보트를 만들었어요.
82. 철수는 책을 읽다가 힘이 들어서 산책을 하러 공원에 나갔습니다.
83. 스마트폰은 우리의 생활을 바꾸어 놓은 테크놀로지다.
84. 맥주를 마시면 배가 부르지만 기분이 좋아진다.
85. 피자는 어린이들만 좋아하는 음식이 아니라, 어른들도 좋아한다.
86. 원숭이가 바나나를 좋아한다는 이야기는 사실이었어!
87. 안경을 잃어버린 철수는 앞이 잘 보이지 않아서 고생 했다.
88. 문장의 의미를 모르면 뜻을 이해하는 게 쉽지 않다.
89. 코끼리가 옆에 있으면, 사람이 정말 작아 보인다. 반대로, 강아지가 옆에 있으면, 사람이 커 보인다.
90. 엄마가 아빠에게 문자를 보냈다. "집에 올때 마트에서 고기를 사오세요."
91. 한국의 여름은 너무 더워서 노인들이 힘들어한다.
92. 기분이 좋지 않으면 노래를 크게 불러보자!
93. 술을 너무 많이 마시면 건강이 나빠진다!
94. 공부를 열심히 하면, 너의 꿈이 이루어 질 거야.
95. 잠을 안자고 스마트폰을 가지고 놀면, 피곤해진다.
96. 소나무에 솔방울이 크게 열렸다. 사다리를 가지고 와서 따볼까?
97. 운동을 너무 열심히 했더니 몸이 피곤하구나.
98. 연습을 많이 해야 실력이 좋아지지.
99. 한글을 공부하면, 한국어 실력이 훨씬 좋아질 거야!
100.   나보다 나이가 많은 사람을 만나면, 예의를 갖춰서 말해야 한다.

PREDICATE
서술어

Q: Which of the following can be used to describe the beach?

바다는... 1) 오늘 2) 아름답다 3) 를 4) 정말 5) 수박

Answer : 2) 아름답다

Predicate (서술어) of a sentence describes and identifies:

1) a person or a thing (place, building, object, and etc.)
2) a movement
3) a shape and the characteristics
4) condition.

Without it, we can't clearly understand what the subject does or what it looks like.

Circle the part that is a predicate.

나는		기쁘다.
거북이는		느리다.
바나나는		맛있다.
야구는	정말	재미있다.

Categorize the following set of 서술어 below.

아름답다   공부하다   학생이다

배고프다   병원입니다   멋지다

달리다   높다   아프다   소년이다

1) Person / Thing

2) Movement

3) Shape and Characteristics

4) Condition

Answer Key

1) 학생이다   병원입니다   소년이다
2) 공부하다   달리다
3) 아름답다   높다   멋지다
4) 배고프다   아프다

Circle the 서술어 to complete the following sentences.

비행기는 매우 | 빠른 | 빨리 | 빠르다. |

철수가 책을 | 조용히 | 큰 | 읽는다. |

강아지가 정말 | 귀엽다. | 다시 | 왜 |

제주도 풍경은 | 왜 | 아름답다. | 한번 |

Answer Key

빠르다.   읽는다.   귀엽다.   아름답다.

Categorize the following set of 서술어 below.

날다   친구다

최고다   학교입니다

뛰다   높다   소녀다

---

1) Identifies a Subject

2) Describes a Movement

3) Describes a Characteristic / Condition

Circle the 서술어 to complete the following sentences.

사자는 매우   빠른   빨리   무섭다.

미호가 밥을   조용히   많이   먹는다.

고양이가 정말   예쁘다.   어디에   왜

겨울은   아름다운   춥다.   한번

Practice writing the following sentences and color the 서술어 portion of the sentence.

철수가 사탕을 먹는다 .

아기피부는 매우 부드럽다 .

피자는 정말 맛있다 .

의자에 앉아서 공부합니다 .

제 이름은 수지입니다 .

Answer Key

먹는다.   부드럽다.   맛있다.   공부합니다.   수지입니다.

Select a 서술어 from the list to complete the following sentences correctly.

좋아합니다.　대학생입니다.　뛰어갑니다.

아픕니다.　김세호입니다.　무섭습니다.

제 이름은
My name is

저는
I am

호랑이가 빠르게
A tiger is (　　　) fast

저는 야구를
I (　　　) baseball.

머리가 많이
My hair (　　　) a lot.

좀비 영화는 정말
Zombie movies are really (　　　).

PREDICATE
서술어

Question 101 - 120. Read the following sentences and identify the portion that has a predicate.

101. 날씨가 춥다. (The weather is cold.)

102. 영희가 청소를 하고 있다. (Yeong-hi is cleaning (the room).)

103. 강아지가 사료를 먹고 있다. (A puppy is eating dog food.)

104. 나무가 매우 크다. (The tree is really big.)

105. 기차가 정말로 길다. (The train is really long.)

106. 독감에 걸려 몸이 아프다. (I'm sick because I have the flu.)

107. 오늘은 정말 졸리다. (I'm really sleepy today.)

108. 아침부터 비가 옵니다. (It's been raining since morning.)

109. 아기가 방긋 웃고 있습니다. (A baby is smiling sweetly.)

110. 제 친구들은 러시아 사람입니다. (My friends are Russians.)

111. 저 건물이 제가 다니는 학교입니다. (That building is the school I go to.)

112. 여기가 바로 광화문입니다. (This is Gwanghwamun right here.)

113. 어제부터 공부를 열심히 하고 있다. (I've been studying hard since yesterday.)

114. 바람이 정말 차갑게 분다. (The wind is blowing really cold.)

115. 운동을 많이 해서 몸이 피곤하다. (I feel tired because I worked out a lot.)

116. 종이를 접어서 예쁜 모양을 만들었다. (I folded a paper into a pretty shape.)

117. 인터넷이 빠르다. (The Internet is fast.)

118. 피아노 소리가 아름답다. (The piano sounds beautiful.)

119. 바이올린 연습은 참 어렵다. (Practicing the violin is very difficult.)

120. 오리와 닭은 생김새가 다르다. (Ducks and chickens have different looks.)

Question 121 - 150. Read the following sentences and identify which of the following their predicates 1) identify a subject 2) describe a movement 3) describe a characteristic / condition. Write down a corresponding number.

121. 나는 학생이다. (I'm a student.)

122. 나의 이름은 김철수다. (My name is Kim Cheol-soo.)

123. 내 친구는 키가 크다. (My friend is tall.)

124. 민호가 책을 읽고 있다. (Min-ho is reading a book.)

125. 기린의 목은 정말 길다. (The neck of a giraffe is really long.)

126. 백화점에 사람들이 정말 많다! (There are really a lot of people in the department store!)

127. 얼룩말이 뛰어간다. (A zebra is running.)

128. 머리가 아프다. (My head hurts.)

129. 구름이 천천히 지나간다. (The clouds are moving past slowly.)

130. 저기 있는 사람이 내 삼촌이야. (That person over there is my uncle.)

131. 전화기가 따르릉 울렸습니다. (The bell rang r-r-ring).

132. 바나나는 노랑색이다. (Bananas are of yellow color.)

133. 철수가 자전거에 앉아서 운동하고 있다. (Cheol-soo is exercising, sitting on a bicycle.)

134. 날씨가 맑다. (The weather is clear.)

135. 바람이 매섭게 불어 춥다. (It's cold because of the fierce weather.)

136. 공부를 하다가 잠들었다. (I fell asleep while stuyding.)

137. 이 커다란 동물이 공룡입니다. (This huge animal is a dinosaur.)

138. 얼룩말이 빠르게 달려간다. (A zebra is running fast.)

139. 휘발유 가격이 비싸다. (The price of gasoline is expansive.)

140. 다이어트를 많이 해서 날씬하다. (I'm slim because of heavy dieting.)

141. 소리가 너무 크다. (The sound is too large (=loud).

142. 라면을 먹었다. (I ate ramyeon.)

143. 라면이 맵다. (Ramyeon is spicy.)

144. 라면이 보글보글 끓는다. (Ramyeon is boiling bubbly.)

145. 도서관에 책이 많다. (There are a lot of books at the library.)

146. 지갑을 잃어버렸다. (I lost a wallet.)

147. 운동은 힘들다. (Working out is difficult.)

148. 책상위에 있는 것은 연필입니다. (What's on the desk is a pencil.)

149. 비행기가 자동차보다 빠르다. (Airplanes are faster than a car.)

150. 한국어 공부는 즐겁다. (Studying Korea is enjoyable.)

Question 151 - 180. Fill in the blanks with the appropriate predicates from the list to complete the following sentences.

```
아프다   고프다   높다   낮다   즐겁다   동물이다

식물이다   달려간다   느리다   책상입니다   길다   달다

펼럭입니다   학생이다   어리다   영화다   이민수입니다   똑같다

다르다   먹고 있다   배부르다   앉았다   많다   선생님이다

호랑이다   날아간다   크다   쉽다   잠들었다   건물이다
```

151. 롯데월드타워는 555미터로, 대한민국에서 가장 높은 (   ).
(Lotte World Tower is the highest (   ) in Korea, at 555 meters.)

152. 눈이 많이 쌓인 길에서 넘어졌더니 엉덩이가 (   ).
(My hips (   ) as I fell on a street where a lot of snow piled up.)

153. 달리기 속도를 비교하면, 거북이가 토끼보다 훨씬 (   ).
(When running speed is compared, turtles are way (   ) than rabbits.)

154. 잠자리가 해바라기꽃 위에 (   ).
(A dragonfly (   ) on top of a sunflower.)

155. 오렌지와 귤은 비슷하게 생겼지만 맛이 (   ).
(Oranges and tangerines look alike but taste (   ).)

156. 오늘 아침 식사를 하지 않았더니 배가 (   ).
(My stomach is (   ) as I skipped breakfast.)

157. 식물의 반대말은 (   ).
(The opposite of a plant is (   ).

158. 나는 열 살이고 너는 다섯 살이니, 네가 나보다 (   ).
(I'm ten years old and you are five years old. It makes you (   ) than me.)

159. 수학, 과학, 영어, 체육 모두 A+를 받는 철수는 똑똑한 (   ).
(Cheol-soo gets all A+ on mathematics, science, English, and PE. He's a smart (   ).

160. 이것은 의자이고, 저것은 (   ).
(This is a chair, and that is (   ).

161. 소금은 짜고, 설탕은 (   ).
(Salt is salty and sugar is (   ).

162. 학생여러분, 반갑다! 내 이름은 김현정이고, 나는 오늘부터 너희들을 가르칠 (   ).
(Students, nice meeting you! My name is Kim Hyeon-jeong, and I'm (   ) who will be teaching you from today.)

163. 반갑습니다. 제 이름은 (   ).
(Nice meeting you. My name is (   ).

164. 짜장면, 탕수육에 디저트까지 먹어서 (   ).
(I'm (   ) because I ate jjajangmyeon, tang-su-yuk, and dessert.)

165. 동물원에서 가장 무서운 동물은 (   ).
(The scariest animal at the zoo is (   ).

166. 코끼리가 긴 코를 이용해서 과일을 (   ).
(An elephant (   ) a fruit using its long nose.)

167. 친구들과 떠나는 여행은 언제나 (   ).
(A trip with friends is always (   ).

168. 기린이 하마보다 키가 훨씬 (   ).
(Giraffes' height is way (   ) than that of hippos.)

169. 와! 종이 비행기가 정말 잘 (   ).
(Wow! paper plane is really (   ) well.)

170. 수업을 많이 빠졌더니 숙제가 정말 (   ).
(Due to skipping so many classes, there's really (   ) homework.)

171. 타이타닉은 내가 가장 좋아하는 헐리우드 (   ).
(Titanic is my favorite Hollywood (   ).

172. 20cm짜리 막대기는 5cm짜리 막대기보다 길이가 (   ).
(A 20cm stick is (   ) than a 5cm stick in length.)

173. 의자가 높은 줄 알았는데 생각보다 많이 (   ).
(I thought the chair was high, but it's a lot (   ) than I thought.)

174. 쌍둥이 형제는 얼굴이 (   ).
(The faces of twin brothers are (   ).

175. 공부를 많이 했더니 생각보다 시험 문제가 (   ).
(Because I studied a lot, the test questions are (   ) than I thought.)

176. 침팬지는 동물이고, 장미는 (   ).
(Chimpanzees are animals, and roses are (   ).

177. 가을 하늘은 정말 (   ).
(Autum sky is really (   ).

178. 너무 피곤해서 나도 모르게 (   ).
(Because I was too tired, I (   ) without realizing.)

179. 태극기가 바람에 (   ).
(Korean flag is (   ) in wind.)

180. 와! 치타가 정말 빠르게 (   ).
(Wow! A cheetah is (   ) really fast!)

Answer Key

101. 날씨가 <u>춥다</u>.
102. 영희가 청소를 <u>하고 있다</u>.
103. 강아지가 사료를 <u>먹고 있다</u>.
104. 나무가 매우 <u>크다</u>.
105. 기차가 정말로 <u>길다</u>.
106. 독감에 걸려 몸이 <u>아프다</u>.
107. 오늘은 정말 <u>졸리다</u>.
108. 아침부터 비가 <u>옵니다</u>.
109. 아기가 방긋 <u>웃고 있습니다</u>.
110. 제 친구들은 러시아 <u>사람입니다</u>.
111. 저 건물이 제가 다니는 <u>학교입니다</u>.
112. 여기가 바로 <u>광화문입니다</u>.
113. 어제부터 공부를 열심히 <u>하고 있다</u>.
114. 바람이 정말 차갑게 <u>분다</u>.
115. 운동을 많이 해서 몸이 <u>피곤하다</u>.
116. 종이를 접어서 예쁜 모양을 <u>만들었다</u>.
117. 인터넷이 <u>빠르다</u>.
118. 피아노 소리가 <u>아름답다</u>.
119. 바이올린 연습은 참 <u>어렵다</u>.
120. 오리와 닭은 생김새가 <u>다르다</u>.
121. 1
122. 1
123. 3
124. 2
125. 3
126. 3
127. 2
128. 3
129. 2
130. 1
131. 2
132. 3
133. 2
134. 3
135. 3
136. 2
137. 1
138. 2
139. 3
140. 3
141. 3
142. 2
143. 3
144. 2
145. 3
146. 2
147. 3
148. 1
149. 3
150. 3
151. 건물이다
152. 아프다
153. 느리다
154. 앉았다
155. 다르다

156. 고프다
157. 동물이다
158. 어리다
159. 학생이다
160. 책상입니다
161. 달다
162. 선생님이다
163. 이민수입니다
164. 배부르다
165. 호랑이다
166. 먹고 있다
167. 즐겁다
168. 크다
169. 날아간다
170. 많다
171. 영화다
172. 길다
173. 낮다
174. 똑같다
175. 쉽다
176. 식물이다
177. 높다
178. 잠들었다
179. 펭귄입니다
180. 달려간다

TYPES OF SENTENCES
문장의 종류

영희야 그동안 ☐ ?

응. 철수야. 참 오랜만이다!

Q: Which of the following best fits the box?

1) 잘 지냈다 2) 잘 지냈어 3) 잘 지내라

Answer : 2) 잘 지냈어

There are many different types of sentences. They can be in the form of explaining, describing, asking, commanding, and expressing. Usually, they end with the following ending.

Explaining and describing: ~다, ~이다, ~입니다, ~요
Asking/Offering: ~까?, ~요?, ~세요?, ~어?, ~니?, ~가요?, ~니까?, ~자, ~죠
Commanding: ~라, ~세요, ~오, ~시오
Expressing: ~나!, ~다!, ~가!

Copy down the following sentences according to their sentence type.

가을에는 단풍이 아름답습니다.

내일 영화보러 갈까요?

티비를 꺼라.

자, 이제 밥을 먹자.

이렇게 아름다울수가!

1+1은 2입니다.

Explaining and describing:

Asking/Offering:

Commanding:

Expressing:

Complete the following sentences by inserting a correct punctuation mark(. / ? / !), and practice writing by copying down the sentences.

철수가 사탕을 먹나요?

눈사람을 함께 만들까?

백두산은 정말 높구나!

라디오 소리를 줄여라.

나는 배가 많이 고프다.

TYPES OF SENTENCES
문장의 종류

Question 180 - 230. Fill in the blanks with the appropriate punctuation marks (. / ? / !). When there are more than one, write down both.

181. 서울의 날씨는 어떤가요( )
(How's the weather in Seoul ( )

182. 휴! 집이 이렇게 멀다니( )
(Phew! Home is this far( )

183. 오늘은 일찍 자거라( )
(Sleep early tonight ( )

184. 야구가 좋니, 축구가 좋니( )
(Do you like baseball or soccer( )

185. 책을 많이 읽으면 두뇌 건강에 좋다( )
(If you read a lot, it's good for your brain health( )

186. 당장 컴퓨터를 끄세요( )
(Turn off the computer right now( )

187. 여기에 온 이유가 뭐니( )
(What's the reason you came here( )

188. 자리에 앉아도 될까요( )
(May I get seated ( )

189. 여기에 앉으세요( )
(Please sit here( )

190. 와! 날씨가 이렇게 추울수가( )
(Wow! How can the weather be so cold( )

191. 소금과 후추는 어디에 있나요( )
(Where is salt and pepper(   )

192. 밥을 먹었으니 이제 집에 갑시다( )
(Let's go home since we ate(   )

193. 시간이 늦었으니 이제 집에 가자( )
(Let's go home since it's late(   )

194. 어머! 정말 예쁜 드레스네( )
(Oh my! It's a really pretty dress(   )

195. 오늘은 일찍 자야겠다. 내일 일찍 일어나야 하니까( )
(I should sleep early because I have to wake up early tomorrow(   )

196. 와! 시간 정말 빨리간다( )
(Wow! Time really flies(   )

197. 지금 몇시지( )
(What time is it now(   )

198. 이 책의 제목이 뭐였더라( )
(What was the name of this book(   )

199. 도서관에서는 조용히 하거라( )
(Be quiet in a library(   )

200. 나도 게임 하면 안돼( )
(Can I play the game too(   )

201. 우유에는 칼슘이 많다( )
(There's a lot of calcium in milk(   )

202. 와! 우리가 이겼다( )
(Yay! We won(   )

203. 축구 경기는 몇시에 끝나나요( )
(What time does the soccer match end(   )

204. 문제를 듣고 정답을 적어보세요( )
(Listen to the question and write down the answer( )

205. 내가 여기에 온 이유가 뭐였지( )
(What was the reason I came here( )

206. 도둑이다! 도둑 잡아라( )
(Thief! Catch the thief( )

207. 오늘 저녁엔 무엇을 먹을까( )
(What should I eat tonight( )

208. 정말 덥다( )
(It's really hot( )

209. 공부를 마치고 영화를 봐야겠다( )
(I should watch a movie after I finish studying( )

210. 그동안 건강히 잘 지내셨나요( )
(Have you been well so far( )

211. 저는 잘 지냈어요( )
(I've been well( )

212. 내일은 날씨가 맑을거래요( )
(Tomorrow is said to be clear( )

213. 지금 몇시나 되었나( )
(What time is it now( )

214. 너 많이 배고프지( )
(You are very hungry, right( )

215. 내일은 뭐하지( )
(What should I do tomorrow( )

216. 철수야! 학교에 늦겠다! 그만 자고 빨리 일어나( )
(Cheol-soo! You will be late for school! Stop sleeping and wake up( )

217. 자, 이제 밥을 먹어볼까( )
(Well, let's eat now, shall we( )

218. 왜냐면 너무 피곤하니까( )
(Because I'm too tired( )

219. 하느님 맙소사( )
(Oh my god( )

220. 이제 집에 가자꾸나( )
(Let's go home now( )

221. 택시는 어디에서 타나요( )
(Where do I catch a taxi( )

222. 낚시는 정말 재미있네요( )
(Fishing is really fun( )

223. 사람들이 많아서 복잡하다( )
(It's crowded because there are a lot of people( )

224. 음악 소리를 줄여주세요( )
(Please turn down the sound of music( )

225. 경찰이다! 꼼짝 마라( )
(It's the police! Don't move( )

226. 차가 온다! 조심해라( )
(Car's approaching! Watch out( )

227. 점심 잘 챙겨 먹었지( )
(You haven't forgotten to have lunch, right( )

228. 오늘은 일찍 자야지( )
(I should sleep early today( )

229. 도대체 이게 뭐야( )
(What in the world is this( )

230. 아니! 어떻게 이런 일이 있을 수가( )
(Oh my! How could this happen( )

230. 아니! 어떻게 이런 일이 있을 수가( )
(Oh my! How could this happen( )

Answer Key

181. ?
182. !
183. . / !
184. ?
185. .
186. . / !
187. ?
188. ?
189. . / !
190. !
191. ?
192. . / !
193. . / !
194. !
195. .
196. !
197. ?
198. ?
199. . / !
200. ?
201. .
202. !
203. ?
204. .
205. ?
206. !
207. ?
208. !
209. .
210. ?
211. .
212. .
213. ?
214. ?
215. ?
216. !
217. ?
218. .
219. !
220. . / !
221. ?
222. . / !
223. . / !
224. . / !
225. !
226. !
227. ?
228. .
229. ! / ?
230. !

IMITATING WORDS
의성어/의태어

Q: Which of the following describes the way the turtle walks?

거북이가 □□□□□ 기어간다 1) 높은 2) 예쁜 3) 엉금엉금

Answer : 3) 엉금엉금

In Korean, there are words that imitate movements and shapes (의태어) and sounds (의성어), to make a sentence sound more realistic. Circle the words that imitate movements and shapes, and use a triangle for words that imitate sounds.

깡총깡총　요리조리　따르릉　보글보글

쿵　우당탕탕　엉금엉금　바둥바둥

울긋불긋　음매음매　살금살금

Answer Key

Imitating movements / shapes - 깡총깡총　요리조리　엉금엉금　바둥바둥　울긋불긋　살금살금
Imitating sounds - 따르릉　보글보글　쿵　우당탕탕　음매음매

Connect the following pictures with right words.

토끼가 [　　　　] 뛰어갑니다.

● 보글보글

비가 [　　　　] 내립니다.

● 으르렁

수프가 [　　　　] 끓습니다.

● 깡총깡총

단풍이 [　　　　] 들었습니다.

● 울긋불긋

호랑이가 [　　　　] 거립니다.

● 따르릉

전화가 [　　　　] 울립니다.

● 주룩주룩

Practice writing the following sentences and color the 의성어/의태어 portion of the sentence.

아기가 응애응애 운다 .

심장이 쿵쿵 뛰어요 .

비둘기가 파닥파닥 날개짓해요 .

키보드를 타닥타닥 쳐요 .

전투기가 슈웅슈웅 날아간다 .

Answer Key

응애응애. 쿵쿵. 파닥파닥. 타닥타닥. 슈웅슈웅

Select a 의성어/의태어 from the list to complete the following sentences correctly.

삐뽀삐뽀　　꽈당　　멍멍　　야옹야옹
꿀꺽꿀꺽　　찰칵찰칵　　쨍그랑

접시가 [　　　] 소리를 내면서 깨졌다.
The dish broke making (　　　　) sound.

앰뷸런스가 [　　　] 하고 빠르게 지나갔다.
Ambulance drove past fast, making (　　　) sound.

사진을 [　　　] 찍어요.
Taking a photo, (　　　).

목이 말라서 물을 [　　　] 마셨어요.
I drank water (　　　) because I was thirsty.

길이 미끄러워서 [　　　] 하고 넘어졌어요.
I fell (　　　), because the road was slippery.

강아지는 [　　　], 고양이는 [　　　].
Dogs go (　　　), cats go (　　　).

접시가 **쨍그랑** 소리를 내면서 깨졌다.　　앰뷸런스가 **삐뽀삐뽀** 하고 빠르게 지나갔다.　　사진을 **찰칵찰칵** 찍어요.
목이 말라서 물을 **꿀꺽꿀꺽** 마셨어요.　　길이 미끄러워서 **꽈당** 하고 넘어졌어요.　　강아지는 **멍멍** 고양이는 **야옹야옹**.

IMITATING WORDS
의성어 / 의태어

Question 231 - 270. Choose the most appropriate imitating word to complete the following sentences.

231. 강아지가 (   ) 짖는다.
(Dog is barking (   ).
A.보글보글 B.멍멍 C.콩콩 D.용용 E.터벅터벅

232. 오리가 (   ) 걸어간다.
(Duck is walking (   ).
A.깡총깡총 B.콩닥콩닥 C.으르렁 D.부르릉 E.뒤뚱뒤뚱

233. 참새가 (   ) 노래한다.
(Swallow is singing/chirping (   ).
A.짹짹 B.야옹 C.쫘당 D.꿀꿀 E.삑삑

234. 자동차가 (   ) 하고 떠나갔다.
(Car drove away (   ).
A.부르릉 B.깡총깡총 C.부들부들 D.키득키득 E.컹컹

235. 시원한 바람이 (   ) 불어왔다.
(Cool wind blew (   ).
A.살랑살랑 B.후르륵 C.삐용삐용 D.따르릉 E.우당탕

236. 진우가 미끄러운 바닥에서 (   ) 넘어졌다.
(Jinwoo fell (   ) on a slippery road.)
A.쫘당 B.보글보글 C.맴맴 D.후다닥 E.느릿느릿

237. 갓난 아기가 (   ) 기어간다.
(An infant is crawling (   ).
A.부들부들 B.깡총깡총 C.엉금엉금 D.화라락 E.가물가물

238. 방울을 (   ) 흔듭니다.
Shaking a bell (   ).
A.딸랑딸랑 B.키득키득 C.엉금엉금 D.깡총깡총 E.탁탁

239. 고양이가 (   ) 하고 웁니다.
Cat is crying (   ).
A.쌩쌩 B.툭툭 C.컹컹 D.삐요 E.야옹

240. 감기에 걸려 (   ) 기침을 했다.
I coughed (   ) because I have a cold.)
A.토닥토닥 B.콜록콜록 C.보글보글 D.드르륵 E. 쾅쾅

241. 발자국 소리가 나지 않게 (   ) 걸었다.
I walked (   ) not to make any sound.)
A.살금살금 B.뚜벅뚜벅 C.깡총깡총 D.터벅터벅 E.헐레벌떡

242. 갑자기 졸음이 몰려와서 (   ) 졸았다.
(Sleepiness rushed in suddenly so I dozed off (   ).
A.주룩주룩 B.꾸벅꾸벅 C.보글보글 D.사뿐사뿐 E.키득키득

243. 전화기가 (   ) 하고 울렸다.
(The phone rang (   ).
A.따르릉 B.맴맴 C.콰르릉 D.휘리릭 E.삐약삐약

244. 병아리가 (   ) 하고 울었다.
(A chicken cried/chirped (   ).
A.삐약삐약 B.꽥꽥 C.뒤뚱뒤뚱 D.파닥파닥 E.꽈당

245. 목이 말라 물을 (   ) 마셨다.
(I drank water (   ) because I was thirsty.)
A.살금살금 B.벌컥벌컥 C.쩝쩝 D.쾅쾅 E.휘리릭

246. 토끼가 (   ) 뛰어갑니다.
(A rabbit is hopping away (   )).
A.부들부들 B.쾅쾅 C.깡총깡총 D.펄럭펄럭 E.삐뽀삐뽀

247. 천둥이 (   ) 친다.
(Thunder stroke (   )).
A.콰르릉 B.와장창 C.쨍그랑 D.우장창 E.달그락

248. 접시를 떨어뜨려 (   ) 하고 깨졌다.
(I dropped the dish and it broke (   )).
A.땡그랑 B.딩동 C.쨍그랑 D.통통 E.탕탕

249. 경찰이 (   ) 하고 총을 발사했다.
(The police shot the gun (   )).
A.통통 B.쿵쿵 C.탁탁 D.콩콩 E.탕탕

250. 김치찌개가 (   ) 끓기 시작했다.
(Kimchi stew started boiling (   )).
A.보글보글 B.부글부글 C.하늘하늘 D.이글이글 E.후루룩

251. 세호가 순두부찌개를 (   ) 거리며 먹기 시작했다.
(Seho started eating sundubu stew making (   ) sound.
A.우당탕 B.쩝쩝 C.착착 D.칙칙 E.흔들흔들

252. 아기 돼지가 (   ) 거리며 밥을 달라고 한다.
(A baby pig is asking for food making (   ) sound.
A.음매 B.꽥꽥 C.꿀꿀 D.꼬끼오 E.왕왕

253. 개구리가 (   ) 뜁니다.
(A frog jumps (   ))
A.뚜벅뚜벅 B.콩콩 C.폴짝폴짝 D.부르릉 E.철썩철썩

254. 하늘에 구름이 (   ) 떠다닌다.
(A cloud in the sky floats around (   )).
A.둥실둥실 B.엉금엉금 C.주룩주룩 D.쓱쓱 E.훨훨

255. 파도가 (   ) 친다.
(The waves are hitting (   ))
A.철썩철썩 B.펄럭펄럭 C.사뿐사뿐 D.둥둥 E.꼬르륵

256. 회전의자를 (   ) 돌린다.
(I'm spinning a swivel chair (   )).
A.생글생글 B.빙글빙글 C.너풀너풀 D.하늘하늘 E.똑딱똑딱

257. 봄이 오니 꽃이 (   ) 피었다.
(Flowers bloomed (   ) as Spring came.)
A.철썩 B.활짝 C.쫑긋 D.풍덩 E.휘휘

258. 방에 들어올 때는 (   ) 노크를 해라.
(Knock (   ) when you come into the room.)
A.탕탕탕 B.톡톡톡 C.똑똑똑 D.콩콩콩 E.쾅쾅쾅

259. 세탁을 했더니 이불이 (   ) 하구나.
(Comforter feels (   ) because I washed it.)
A.쌩쌩 B.통통 C.팡팡 D.뽀송뽀송 E.푸석푸석

260. 어린 아이가 넘어져서 (   ) 하고 울었다.
(A little kid fell and cried (   )).
A.토닥토닥 B.키득키득 C.하하 D.꺄악 E.으앙

261. 갓난 아이가 (   ) 자고 있다.
(An infant is sleeping (   )).
A.콕콕 B.새근새근 C.두근두근 D.하하 E.냠냠

262. 무서운 영화를 보았더니 심장이 (   ) 뛴다.
(My heart is beating (   ) because I watched a scary movie.)
A.키득키득 B.쎄액쎄액 C.통통 D.쏙쏙 E.두근두근

263. 하늘의 별들이 (　　　) 빛난다.
(Stars in the sky are shining (　)).
A.따르릉　B.반짝반짝　C.울긋불긋　D.하늘하늘　E.깜빡깜빡

264. 지리산에 단풍이 (　　　) 들었다.
(Leaves are changing colors (　) in Jiri Mt.)
A.울긋불긋　B.토실토실　C.느릿느릿　D.하늘하늘　E.살랑살랑

265. 젊은 여자가 구두를 신고 (　　　) 걸었다.
(A young lady walked (　　), wearing shoes.)
A.토실토실　B.살랑살랑　C.토닥토닥　D.찰칵찰칵　E.또각또각

266. 친구들끼리 함께 모여서 사진을 (　　　) 찍었다.
(Took a photo (　) with friends gathered together.)
A.딩동　B.부들부들　C.들락날락　D.찰칵찰칵　E.사뿐사뿐

267. 화가 나서 몸이 (　　　) 떨린다.
(Body is shaking (　) because of anger.)
A.꼬르륵　B.듬성듬성　C.부들부들　D.비틀비틀　E.보글보글

268. 술에 취한 사람이 (　　　) 걷는다.
(A drunk person is walking (　　)).
A.나풀나풀　B.지글지글　C.보들보들　D.꼬불꼬불　E.비틀비틀

269. 후라이팬에 삼겹살을 (　　　) 구워요.
(Grill samgyeopsal (　) on a frying pan.)
A.들쑥날쑥　B.지글지글　C.휘리릭　D.토실토실　E.후두둑

270. 살찐 토끼 엉덩이가 (　　　) 하다.
(A chbby rabbit's buttocks are (　)).
A.토실토실　B.토닥토닥　C.하늘하늘　D.살랑살랑　E.사뿐사뿐

Answer Key

231. B
232. E
233. A
234. A
235. A
236. A
237. C
238. A
239. E
240. B
241. A
242. B
243. A
244. A
245. B
246. C
247. A
248. C
249. E
250. A
251. B
252. C
253. C
254. A
255. A
256. B
257. B
258. C
259. D
260. E
261. B
262. E
263. B
264. A
265. E
266. D
267. C
268. E
269. B
270. A

ADJECTIVES
형용사

맛있고 몸에 좋은 샐러드를 만들었어요.

샐러드를 만들었어요.

Q: Which of the chefs above described their cuisine better?

In Korean, adjectives 형용사 are used to describe the following word more accurately and vividly. Depending on the word you choose, the meaning of a sentence would change drastically.

There are three possible uses of adjectives.

Describing a subject
멋진 **자동차가** 지나갑니다.

Describing an object
선미가 **무서운 영화를** 봅니다.

Describing a predicate
핫도그를 **맛있게 먹었다**.

형용사

Identify the type (describing a subject / an object / a predicate) of the following sentences

1. 빨간 드레스가 아름답네요.
The red dress is beautiful.

2. 우리는 재밌는 영화를 보았다.
We watched a fun movie.

3. 비행기가 빠르게 날아간다.
Airplane is flying fast.

4. 커다란 곰이 고기를 먹는다.
A large bear is eating meat.

5. 기차가 천천히 멈추었다.
A train stopped slowly.

6. 엄마가 맛있는 요리를 해주셨다.
Mom made a delicious dish.

Answer Key

1. Subject 2. Object 3. Predicate 4. Subject 5. Predicate 6. Object

Practice writing the following sentences and color the 형용사 portion of the sentence.

| 하 | 얀 | | 눈 | 사 | 람 | 을 | | 만 | 들 | 어 | 요 | . | | | |

| 오 | 늘 | 은 | | 늦 | 게 | | 일 | 어 | 났 | 어 | 요 | . | | | |

| 재 | 밌 | 는 | | 영 | 화 | 가 | | 좋 | 아 | . | | | | | |

Answer Key

하얀.   늦게.   재밌는.

Connect the adjectives that are opposite in meaning.

커다란 ●

● 깨끗한

더러운 ●

● 느리게

빠르게 ●

● 적은

많은 ●

● 빨리

높은 ●

● 작은

천천히 ●

● 낮은

Select a 형용사 from the list to complete the following sentences correctly.

똑똑한　　좁은　　시원한
매운　　하얗게　　가깝게

제 옆으로 와서 [　　] 앉으세요.
Please come next to me and sit (　　).

[　　] 철수가 수학 시험에서 A를 받았다.
(　　) Cheol-soo got an A on the math test.

[　　] 골목길을 지나면 저희 집이 나와요.
After passing (　　) alley, you will see my house.

추운 겨울에 눈이 [　　] 내렸어요.
Snow came down (　　) in the cold weather.

선풍기에서 [　　] 바람이 불어와요.
(　　) wind is blowing from the fan.

떡볶이는 정말 [　　] 음식이에요.
Tteokbokki is a really (　　) food.

Answer Key

제 옆으로 와서 가깝게 앉으세요.　　똑똑한 철수가 수학 시험에서 A를 받았다.　　좁은 골목길을 지나면 저희 집이 나와요.
추운 겨울에 눈이 하얗게 내렸어요.　　선풍기에서 시원한 바람이 불어와요.　　떡볶이는 정말 매운 음식이에요.

ADJECTIVES
형용사

Question 271 - 320. Choose the most appropriate adjective to complete the following sentences.

271. ( ) 커피를 마시니 몸이 따뜻해졌다.
(I feel warm as I drink ( ) coffee.)
A.따뜻한 B.예쁜 C.잘생긴 D.미운 E.커다란

272. 독수리가 ( ) 날개를 흔듭니다.
(A ( ) eagle is waving its wings.)
A.귀여운 B.커다란 C.매콤한 D.달콤한 E.복잡한

273. 페르시안 카페트는 ( ) 문양이 특징이다.
(A ( ) pattern is the distnict characteristic of Persian carpet.)
A.순수한 B.홀가분한 C.복잡한 D.상냥한 E.힘센

274. 자동차가 ( ) 떠나갔다.
(The car drove away ( ).)
A.재밌게 B.신나게 C.기분좋게 D.달콤하게 E.빠르게

275. 요리가 정말 ( ) 만들어졌다.
(Dish/cuisine has been ( ) prepared.)
A.맛있게 B.무섭게 C.친절하게 D.즐겁게 E.슬프게

276. 우리는 ( ) 영화를 봐서 기분이 좋았다.
(We watched a ( ) movie and that made us feel good.)
A.뜨거운 B.매운 C.재밌는 D.작은 E.빠른

277. ( ) 하늘에는 구름이 한 점 없구나.
(A ( ) sky has not a single cloud.)
A.누런 B.빨간 C.파란 D.잘생긴 E.비참한

278. (   ) 장미가 참 아름답구나.
(A (   ) rose is really beautiful.)
A.달콤한 B.친한 C.상쾌한 D.빨간 E.네모난

279. (   ) 사탕을 많이 먹으면 이가 썩는다.
(Eating (   ) candies will give you cavities.)
A.달콤한 B.매콤한 C.즐거운 D.상냥한 E.아픈

280. 당신의 (   ) 배려심에 감사합니다.
(Thank you for your (   ) consideration.)
A.건강한 B.매력적인 C.상냥한 D.허황된 E.빠른

281. 너무 (   ) 선물을 사주셔서 부담스럽네요.
(I feel uncomfortable because you bought me a gift that's too (   ).
A.추운 B.비싼 C.건전한 D.신비로운 E.급한

282. 강아지는 인간의 가장 (   ) 친구다.
(Dogs are most (   ) friends to humans.)
A.무서운 B.평범한 C.친한 D.두꺼운 E.높은

283. 백두산은 대한민국에서 가장 (   ) 산입니다.
(Mt. Baekdu is the (   ) mountain in Korea.
A.따가운 B.부드러운 C.네모난 D.높은 E.부족한

284. 아보카도는 영양이 (   ) 식품입니다.
(Avocado is a food (   ) in nutrition.)
A.풍부한 B.부족한 C.하찮은 D.타고난 E.커다란

285. 우리 할머니는 (   ) 이야기를 많이 알고계신다.
(My grandmother knows a lot of (   ) stories.)
A.시끄러운 B.재미난 C.어지러운 D.추운 E.따스한

286. (   ) 거인이 쿵쿵거리며 걸어갑니다.
(A giant is walking around making (   ) sound.)
A.부족한 B.낮은 C.미안한 D.거대한 E.거룩한

287. 성당은 (   ) 장소이다.
(Church is a (   ) place.)
A.신성한 B.촘촘한 C.팽팽한 D.깊은 E.신나는

288. 과학으로도 설명하기 힘든 (   ) 현상이다.
(It's a (   ) phenomenon hard to explain even with science.)
A.지겨운 B.겁나는 C.진지한 D.신기한 E.평범한

289. 아무 특징도 없는, (   ) 제품입니다.
(It's a (   ) product that has no distinct features.)
A.특별한 B.평범한 C.특이한 D.유사한 E.희귀한

290. 어린이의 (   ) 눈을 보면 마음이 편해진다.
(Looking at the (   ) eyes of children makes me feel comfortable.)
A.순수한 B.미련한 C.어이없는 D.근심어린 E.매서운

291. 축구는 매우 (   ) 스포츠다.
(Soccer is a very (   ) sport.)
A.격렬한 B.반가운 C.철저한 D.똑똑한 E.매콤한

292. 오랜만에 만난 친구의 얼굴에 (   ) 표정이 가득했다.
(My friend who I'haven't seen in a while had (   ) looks full on his face.)
A.훌륭한 B.어지러운 C.배고픈 D.반가운 E.시끄러운

293. (   ) 소리에 놀라 잠에서 깼다.
(I woke up startled, to a (   ) sound.)
A.맑은 B.부드러운 C.시끄러운 D.자유로운 E.해맑은

294. 겨울에는 (   ) 육개장이 최고야.
(During the winter, (   ) yukgaejang is the best.)
A.얼큰한 B.비릿한 C.어설픈 D.신랄한 E.안전한

295. 위험합니다! 모두 (   ) 곳으로 이동하세요.
(Dangerous! Everybody move to a (   ) place.)
A.안전한 B.위험한 C.가까운 D.따뜻한 E.추운

296. (   ) 자세로 오래 앉았더니 허리가 아프다.
(My back hurts after sitting in a (   ) position for a long time.)
A.유연한 B.부드러운 C.불편한 D.괜찮은 E.빈번한

297. (   ) 사막은 비가 내리지 않아 끔찍한 모습이었다.
(   ) desert looked horrible due to not raining.)
A.매마른 B.질긴 C.쫄깃한 D.부드러운 E.추운

298. 어린이들의 (   ) 미소를 보면 행복해진다.
(Looking at the (   ) smile of children makes me happy.)
A.방탕한 B.경직된 C.착잡한 D.두려운 E.해맑은

299. 로보트는 (   ) 움직임이 특징이다.
(   ) movements are a distnict characteristic of robots.)
A.나태한 B.즐거운 C.현명한 D.날카로운 E.경직된

300. 수미와 현수는 색깔이 (   ) 옷을 입었다.
(Sumi and Hyeonsu wore clothes that are (   ) in color.)
A.거칠은 B.똑똑한 C.비슷한 D.가파른 E.높은

301. (   ) 포도가 참 맛있겠다.
(   ) grape looks really tasty.)
A.싱싱한 B.생생한 C.미끄러운 D.매운 E.독한

302. 민수는 어제 밤에 (   ) 꿈을 꾸었다.
(Minsu had a (   ) dream last night.)
A.커다란 B.생생한 C.통통한 D.피곤한 E.날카로운

303. 과일을 깎을 때는 (   ) 칼을 조심해라.
(Be careful with the (   ) knife when peeling an apple.)
A.느끼한 B.싱싱한 C.좋은 D.날카로운 E.침침한

304. 감옥에서 풀려난 죄수는 (   ) 삶을 살았다.
(The prisoner who's been released from jail lived a (   ) life.)
A.해로운 B.화가난 C.두려운 D.지곤한 E.자유로운

305. 모기와 파리는 인간에게 (   ) 벌레다.
(Mosquitoes and flies are vermins (   ) to humans.)
A.의로운 B.이로운 C.해로운 D.미안한 E.유사한

306. 친구들이 모두 떠나간 후, 그는 (   ) 삶을 살았다.
(After all of his friends left, he lived a (   ) life.)
A.빠듯한 B.추운 C.외로운 D.의로운 E.이로운

307. 옳은 일을 많이 하는 사람은 (   ) 사람이다.
(A person who does a lot of right things is a (   ) person.)
A.힘찬 B.피곤한 C.연로한 D.괴로운 E.의로운

308. 영화배우가 (   ) 의상을 입고 시상식에 나타났다.
(A movie actor appeared on an award event wearing (   ) clothes.)
A.사악한 B.착한 C.싱싱한 D.희미한 E.화려한

309. 나는 부드러운 고기보다 (   ) 고기가 더 좋다.
(I like (   ) meat better than soft meat.)
A.질긴 B.동그란 C.둥그런 D.작은 E.커다란

310. 한국어는 정말 (   ) 언어야!
(Korean is a really (   ) language!)
A.따가운 B.어려운 C.희망적인 D.습한 E.매끄러운

311. (   ) 시민들이 광장으로 모여들어 시위를 시작했다.
(   ) citizens gathered at the plaza and started protesting.)
A.성난 B.행복한 C.궁금한 D.기괴한 E.어설픈

312. 10시간 동안 비행기를 타는 것은 정말 (   ) 경험이었다.
(Flying on an airplane for 10 hours was a really (   ) experience.)
A.따가운 B.지루한 C.매서운 D.간지러운 E.취한

313. (   ) 사람은 살을 빼기 위해서 다이어트를 한다.
(   ) person goes on a diet to lose fat.)
A.건강한 B.초라한 C.심심한 D.뚱뚱한 E.귀여운

314. (   ) 사람은 거짓말을 하지 않는다.
(   ) person does not lie.)
A.솔직한 B.유명한 C.무식한 D.유식한 E.유익한

315. 르네상스 시대의 (   ) 조각상을 보니 감탄이 나온다.
(Looking at the (   ) statues from the Renaissance period makes me awe.)
A.무모한 B.정교한 C.무딘 D.날카로운 E.두터운

316. 아프리카에서 가장 (   ) 동물은 사자다.
(The most (   ) animal in Africa is a lion.)
A.창백한 B.행복한 C.용맹한 D.미운 E.힘없는

317. (   ) 빙판길을 지날 때에는 조심히 걸어야 한다.
(When passing by a (   ) frozen road, you need to walk carefully.)
A.껄끄러운 B.반들반들한 C.미끄러운 D.사나운 E.형편없는

318. 어려운 문제들을 다 풀고 나니, (   ) 문제들만 남았네.
(After solving all the difficult questions, only (   ) questions are left.)
A.건방진 B.빠듯한 C.헐거운 D.나태한 E.쉬운

319. (   ) 몸매를 유지하려면 살찌는 음식을 먹지 말아야 한다.
(To maintain a (   ) body, you shouldn't eat fattening food.)
A.날씬한 B.우스운 C.게으른 D.부지런한 E.희망찬

320. (   ) 표정을 하고 있는 환자들을 보니 마음이 아팠다.
(After seeing patients with (   ) faces, I felt heart broken.)
A.괴로운 B.마른 C.우스운 D.가뿐한 E.은근한

Answer Key

271. A
272. B
273. C
274. E
275. A
276. C
277. C
278. C
279. A
280. C
281. B
282. C
283. D
284. A
285. B
286. D
287. A
288. D
289. B
290. A
291. A
292. D
293. C
294. A
295. A
296. C
297. A
298. E
299. E
300. C
301. A
302. B
303. D
304. E
305. C
306. C
307. E
308. E
309. A
310. B
311. A
312. B
313. D
314. A
315. B
316. C
317. C
318. E
319. A
320. A

Q: Who introduced oneself using 존대말?

1) 제니 2) 마이클 3) 미효 4) 토니

Answer : 3) 미효

In Korean, if someone being talked to/about is an older person, a stranger of roughly equal or greater age, an employer, a teacher, a customer, and the like, honorifics are used to reflect the speaker's relationship to the subject of the sentence.

In general, 존대말 can be made by using 1) honorific nouns and 2) honorific verbs/predicates.

Let's take a look at some of the common examples.

HONORIFIC NOUNS

One way of using honorifics is to use special "honorific" nouns in place of regular ones. A common example is using 진지 instead of 밥 for "food". Often, honorific nouns are used to refer to relatives. The honorific suffix -님 is affixed to many kinship terms to make them honorific. Thus, someone may address his own grandmother as 할머니 but refer to someone else's grandmother as 할머님.

HONORIFIC VERBS

All verbs and adjectives can be converted into an honorific form by adding the infix -시- or -으시- after the stem and before the ending. Thus, 가다 ("to go") becomes 가시다.

A few verbs have suppletive humble forms, used when the speaker is referring to him/herself in polite situations. These include 드리다 and 올리다 for 주다 ("give"). 드리다 is substituted for 주다 when the latter is used as an auxiliary verb, while 올리다 (literally "raise up") is used for 주다 in the sense of "offer".

Base Form Verb	Honorific Form Verb
공부하다	공부합니다
학생이다	학생입니다 / 학생이에요
보아라	보세요
뛰어라	뛰세요

Base Form Verb	Honorific Form Verb
집	댁
나이	연세
밥	진지
나	저
아빠	아버지

Base Form Verb	Honorific Form Verb
보았니?	보셨나요?
읽었니?	읽으셨나요?
하니?	하십니까?
달리니?	달리십니까?

Select an honorific from the list to complete the following sentences correctly.

댁에   께서   드세요
드렸다   앉으세요   보셨나요

다리 아프실텐데 여기에 ☐ .
Your legs must hurt. Please ( ) here.

할아버지 ☐ 가서 저녁을 먹고 왔다.
I went to grandfather's ( ) and had dinner.

어머니 ☐ 요리를 해 주셨다.
Mother made a ( ) meal.

선생님! 이 영화 ☐ ?
Teacher! Have you ( ) this movie?

할머니, 국이 뜨거우니 천천히 ☐ .
Grandmother, the soup is hot so ( ) slowly.

어머니께 선물을 ☐ .
I ( ) gift to mother.

Connect the normal words with the correct honorific forms.

밥 ●	● 연세
나이 ●	● 잡수시다
나 ●	● 여쭙다
먹다 ●	● 생신
묻다 ●	● 진지
생일 ●	● 저

Answer Key

밥-진지   나이-연세   나-저   먹다-잡수시다   묻다-여쭙다   생일-생신

HONORIFICS
높임말/존대말

Question 321 - 340. Choose the most appropriate honorifics to complete the following sentences.

321. 아버지, 점심 (   ) 하셨어요?
(Father, did you (   ) lunch?)
A.까까 B.밥 C.냠냠 D.식사 E.먹기

322. 할아버지, 이쪽에 (   )
(Grandfather, please (   ) over here.)
A.앉아라. B.앉을래? C.앉으세요. D.앉으렴. E.앉아봐.

323. 선생님, 많이 가르쳐 주셔서 (   ).
(Teacher, (   ) for teaching me a great deal.)
A.감사드린다 B.고맙구나 C.감사합니다 D.고맙네 E.감사해

324. 의사 선생님, 저는 감기에 걸려서 머리가 (   ).
(Doctor, my head (   ) because I have a cold.)
A.아픕니다 B.아프네 C.아픈데 D.아프다 E.아프구나

325. 할머니, (   ) 잡수셨어요?
(Grandmother, did you have (   )?)
A.먹이 B.진지 C.먹을 것 D.밥 E.아침밥

326. 죄송하지만 젓가락 좀 (   )
(I'm sorry, but could you please (   ) chopsticks?)
A.가져와. B.주거라. C.주시겠니? D.주시겠어요? E.내놓을래?

327.할아버지 (   )에 가서 인사드려야지.
(I should go pay a visit to where my grandfather (   ).
A.먹는 곳 B.사는 곳 C.있는 곳 D.집 E.댁

328. 김 선생님께서는 저쪽에 (   )
(Mr. Kim (   ) right over there.)
A.있지. B.있지? C.계십니다. D.있다. E.있습니다.

329. 내가 선생님께 (   ).
(I will (   ) the teacher.)
A.물어볼게 B.여쭤볼게 C.말할게 D.물을게 E.말해볼게

330. 아버지께 선물을 (   ).
(   ) the gift to my father.)
A.줬다 B.줘라 C.드려라 D.건네라 E.주거라

331. 어머니, 용돈 좀 (   )
(Mom, please (   ) some allowance.)
A.주세요. B.줘라. C.줘. D.드려요. E.드려.

332. 선생님, 이 책 읽어 (   )
(Teacher, have you (   ) this book?)
A.봤냐? B.보았어? C.보셨어요? D.봤지? E.봤겠지?

333. 할아버지, 안녕히 (   )
(Grandfather, (   ) well?)
A.잤지요? B.자셨어요? C.잤죠? D.주무셨어요? E.잤어요?

334. 기사 아저씨, 이번 정류장에 (   )
(Mr. driver, (   ) at this stop.)
A.내려주세요. B.내려주라. C.내려주렴. D.내려주겠니. E.내린다.

335. 어서들 오셔서 식사 (   )
(Everybody come quick and (   ) a meal.)
A.해 B.하거라 C.하렴 D.하세요 E.하셔라

336. 어르신, 서두르지 마시고 천천히 (   ).
(Sir, do not rush and (   ) slowly.)
A.오세요 B.오렴 C.와요 D.오시렴 E.와라

337. 신사 숙녀 여러분, 모두 자리에서 (   ).
(Ladies and gentlemen, please (   ) from the seat.)
A.일어나거라 B.일어나시라 C.일어나십시오 D.일어나시오 E.일어나

338. 할아버지, 하루에 한 번, 식사 후에 (   )
(Grandfather, (   ) once a day, after a meal.)
A.먹어라 B.드시라 C.드세요 D.먹으세요 E.드셔라

339. 아버지, 친구랑 비디오 게임을 해도 (   )
(Father, may I (   ) the video game with my friend?)
A.돼? B.될까? C.될까요? D.되겠지? E.되지?

340. 손님 여러분, 빨리 짐을 (   ).
(Dear guests, (   ) your luggage quickly.
A.챙기자 B.챙기세요 C.챙기거라 D.챙겨 E.챙겨라

Question 341 - 400. Correct the underlined parts with the misused honorifics into a normal form.

341. 철수가 밥을 <u>드신다</u>.
(Cheol-soo is having a meal.)

342. 선생님! <u>제가</u> 문제를 <u>푸시겠습니다</u>.
(Teacher! I will solve the problem.)

343. 내가 제일 먼저 집에 <u>오셨다</u>.
(I came home first.)

344. 내 동생이 열심히 운동을 하고 <u>계시다</u>.
(My little brother/sister is working out hard.)

345. 예쁜 여자 아이가 <u>태어나셨다</u>.
(A pretty girl has been born.)

346. 나는 다리가 아파서 자리에 <u>앉으셨다</u>.
(I sat down because my legs hurt.)

347. 할아버지, <u>내가</u> 해드릴게요.
(Grandfather, I will do it for you.)

348. 할아버지<u>에게</u> 선물을 드렸다.
(I gave a gift to grandfather.)

349. 선생님<u>의</u> 나에게 숙제를 내주셨다.
(Teacher gave me homework.)

350. 페르시안 카페트는 정교한 문양이 특징<u>이십니다</u>.
(Elaborate patterns are the distinct feature of Persian carpet.)

351. 자동차<u>께서</u> 빠르게 <u>떠나가셨다</u>.
(A car drove away fast.)

352. 요리가 정말 맛있게 <u>만들어지셨다</u>.
(Meal has been prepared really deliciously.)

353. 우리는 재밌는 영화를 <u>보셔서</u> 기분<u>께서</u> 좋았다.
(We became happy because we watched a fun movie.)

354. <u>따뜻하신</u> 커피를 마시니 몸<u>께서</u> <u>따뜻해지셨다</u>.
(My body became warm after drinking a warm coffee.)

355. 독수리가 커다란 날개를 <u>흔드십니다</u>.
(An eagle is waving its large wings.)

356. 햄버거와 피자는 패스트푸드<u>이십니다</u>.
(Hamburger and pizza are fast foods.)

357. 강아지<u>께서</u> 꼬리를 <u>흔드십니다</u>.
(A puppy is waging its tail.)

358. 호랑이가 고기를 <u>드십니다</u>.
(A tiger is eating meat.)

359. 무지개에는 일곱 색깔이 <u>있으십니다</u>.
(There are seven colors in a rainbow.)

360. 나는 배가 <u>고프시다</u>.
(I'm hungry.)

Question 361 - 370. Convert the following sentences into an honorific form.

361. 어머니가 나에게 용돈을 주었다.
(Mother gave me allownace.)

362. 할머니와 할아버지가 밥을 먹는다.
(Grandmother and granfather are eating a meal.)

363. 아버지가 강아지에게 먹이를 준다.
(Father is feeding a puppy.)

364. 선생님이 나를 칭찬 해줬다.
(Teacher complimented me.)

365. 할아버지가 의자에 앉아있다.
(Grandfather is sitting on a chair.)

366. 삼촌이 나와 놀아줬다.
(Uncle played with me.)

367. 내 이름은 박민호다.
(My name is Park Min Ho.)

368. 고모부가 티비를 본다.
(Uncle is watching TV.)

369. 외삼촌이 농구를 한다.
(Uncle is playing basketball.)

370. 이모가 요리를 하고 있다.
(Aunt is cooking.)

321. D
322. C
323. C
324. A
325. B
326. D
327. E
328. C
329. B
330. C
331. A
332. C
333. D
334. A
335. D
336. A
337. C
338. C
339. C
340. B
341. 드신다 – 먹는다
342. 푸시겠습니다 – 풀겠습니다
343. 오셨다 – 왔다
344. 계시다 – 있다
345. 태어나셨다 – 태어났다
346. 앉으셨다 – 앉았다
347. 내가 – 제가
348. 할아버지에게 – 할아버지께
349. 선생님이 – 선생님께서
350. 특징이십니다 – 특징이다
351. 자동차께서 – 자동차가 , 떠나가셨다 – 떠나갔다
352. 만들어지셨다 – 만들었다
353. 보셔서 – 봐서 , 기분께서 – 기분이
354. 따뜻하신 – 따뜻한 , 몸께서 – 몸이 , 따뜻해지셨다 – 따
뜻해졌다
355. 흔드습니다 – 흔듭니다
356. 패스트푸드이십니다 – 패스트푸드입니다
357. 강아지께서 – 강아지가 , 흔드십니다 – 흔듭니다
358. 드십니다 – 먹습니다
359. 있으십니다 – 있습니다
360. 고프시다 – 고프다
361. 어머니께서 나에게 용돈을 주셨다.
362. 할머니니와 할머니께서 진지를 잡수신다 (식사를 드
신다).
363. 아버지께서 강아지에게 먹이를 주신다.
364. 선생님께서 나를 칭찬 해주셨다.
365. 할아버지께서 의자에 앉아계시다.
366. 삼촌께서 나와 놀아주셨다.
367. 제 이름은 박민호입니다.
368. 고모부께서 티비를 보신다.
369. 외삼촌께서 농구를 하신다.
370. 이모께서 요리를 하고 계시다.

우리는 내년에
대학생이
_____.

Q: Which of the following should go in the blank?

1) 되고있어요 2) 되었어요 3) 될거예요

Answer : 3) 될거예요

When writing sentences, you can talk about something that's already happened (past), happening now (present) and is going to happen (future).

Let's take a look at some of the common examples and answer the following set of questions.

HOW \ WHEN	Already Happened	Happening Now	Going To Happen
By Changing Prediate Portion	Use ~ 앗, ~었 in predicates	Use ~ 고있다 in predicates	Use ~ 을것이다, ~겠다 in predicates
	먹다 -> 먹었다 보다 -> 보았다 읽다 -> 읽었다 놀다 -> 놀았다	먹다 -> 먹고있다 보다 -> 보고있다 읽다 -> 읽고있다 놀다 -> 놀고있다	먹다 -> 먹을것이다 보다 -> 보겠다 읽다 -> 읽을것이다 놀다 -> 놀겠다
By Using Words Describing Time	어제 그저께 작년 지난 주	지금 요즈음	앞으로 다음에 내일 모레 내년

87

Connect the following sentences with the correct time form.

친구와 밥을 먹고 있다. ●

공부를 열심히 했다. ●

● Already Happened

학교에 가고 있다. ●

● Happening Now

친구와 영화를 볼 것이다. ●

● Will Happen

눈이 많이 내렸다. ●

30분 후에 집에 갈거야. ●

Answer Key

Already Happened - 공부를 열심히 했다.   눈이 많이 내렸다.
Happening Now - 친구와 밥을 먹고 있다.   학교에 가고 있다.
Will Happen - 친구와 영화를 볼 것이다.   30분 후에 집에 갈거야.

Select an expression from the list to complete the following sentences correctly.

지금　어제　내일
3일 전에　5년 후에　방금

밤에 친구네 집에서 잤다.
I slept over at my friend's (　　) night.

읽고 있는 책의 제목이 뭐니?
What's the name of the book you are reading (　　)?

아침 9시에는 일어나야 한다.
I have to wake up at least at nine (　　) morning.

막 학교에 도착했어요.
I (　　) got to school now.

우리가 갔던 레스토랑 이름이 뭐였지?
What was the name of the restaurant we went to (　　)?

나는 어떤 모습일까?
What would I look like (　　)?

PAST / PRESENT / FUTURE
시간의 표현

Question 371 - 390. Choose the most appropriate expression to complete the following sentences.

371. 동훈아, 내일 뭐 (   )
(Dong-hoon, what are you (   ) tomorrow?)
A.먹고 있어? B.먹었어? C.먹고 있니? D.먹을 거니? E.먹는구나?

372. 어제는 날씨가 매우 (   )
(It was very (   ) yesterday.)
A.춥겠지? B.춥구나. C.추웠다. D.추울 것 같다. E.춥다.

373. 나는 지금 공부를 (   )
(I'm (   ) now.)
A.하고 있어. B.했었어. C.했다. D.하고 있었다. E.하자.

374. 내년 겨울에는 하와이로 (   )
(   ) to Hawaii next winter.
A.여행가자. B.여행했어? C.여행하고 있다. D.여행했다. E.여행 중이다.

375. 영희는 지금 학교에 (   )
(Yeong-hee is now (   ) to school.)
A.갔다. B.갔었다. C.가고 있었다. D.가고 있다. E.갔었지?

376. 어제 먹은 불고기는 정말 (   )
(The bulgogi we ate yesterday was really (   ).
A.맛있었다. B.맛있다. C.맛있겠지? D.맛있겠다. E.맛있지?

377. 내일 1시까지 그 곳으로 (   )
(I (   ) there by 1 o'clock tomorrow.)
A.갔어. B.갈게. C.가고 있어. D.가고 있습니다. E.갔다.

378. 3일 전에, 예쁜 강아지 5마리가 (   )
(5 pretty puppies (   ) 3 days ago.)
A.태어난다. B.태어납니다. C.태어나셨다. D.태어났다. E.태어나고 있었다.

379. 철수는 지금 배가 너무 고파서 혼자서 밥을 (   )
(Cheol-soo (   ) a meal alone now because he is too hungry.)
A.먹습니까? B.먹었을까? C.먹었었습니다. D.먹고 있습니다. E.먹었습니다.

380. 지난 여름은 정말 더웠다. 내년 겨울은 (   )
(Last summer was really hot. Winter next year (   )
A.추울까? B.추웠다. C.추웠었어? D.추운 중이다. E.추웠지?

381. 어제 본 영화는 정말 (   )
(The movie we watched last night was really (   ).
A.무섭겠지? B.무서울까? C.무섭겠다. D.무섭다. E.무서웠다.

382. 2060년에는 얼마나 멋진 테크놀로지가 (   )
(What kind of cool technology (   ) in year 2060?)
A.생길까? B.생겼네. C.생겼었지? D.생겼다. E.생기고 있을까?

383. 내일 우리가 (   ) 장소는 어디인가요?
(Where is the place we are (   ) tomorrow?)
A.만났던 B.만난 C. D.식사 E.만날

384. 저는 커서 과학자가 되고 (   )
(I want to (   ) a scientist when I grow up.)
A.싫습니다. B.싫다. C.싫었다. D.싫을까? E.싫네.

385. 우리 내일은 무엇을 (   )
(What (   ) tomorrow?)
A.한다. B.할까? C.하자. D.하네. E.했지?

386. 내일은 비가 그치고 바람이 많이 (   )
(It will stop raining and a lot of wind (   ) tomorrow.)
A.불었다. B.불고 있다. C.불겠습니다. D.부는 중이다. E.불었었다.

387. 어제는 비가 하루종일 (   )
(It (   ) all day long yesterday.)
A.내릴 예정이다. B.내릴 것이다. C.내린다. D.내렸다. E.내리고 있었다.

388. 내일 저녁에는 맛있는 불고기를 (   )
(Tomorrow night I should (   ) the tasty bulgogi.)
A.먹어야지. B.먹었다. C.먹었지? D.먹었니? E.먹고 있다.

389. 내일부터 열심히 운동을 (   )
(I will (   ) hard starting tomorrow.)
A.했었다. B.했다. C.한다. D.하겠다. E.하고 있다.

390. 5년 전 오늘, 나는 이곳에서 공부를 (   )
(5 years ago today, I (   ) here.)
A.하다. B.한다. C.했다. D.하렴. E.하지.

Question 391 - 400. Choose the most appropriate answer to fill in the blanks.

391. A: 내일 아침에 뭐 할 거야? (What are you doing tomorrow morning?)
　　B: 일찍 일어나서 공부 (   ) (Wake up early and (   ))

A.했어. B.했었지. C.해야지. D.하고 있어. E.했습니다.

392. A: 축구 경기 벌써 끝났어? (Did the soccer match end already?)
　　B: 응. 우리나라가 3:1로 (   ) (Yes. We (   ) 3:1.)

A.이기고 있어. B.이긴다. C.이길거야! D.이겼어. E.이길 것 같아.

393. A: 한국에서 뭐하고 있어? (What are you doing in Korea?)
　　B: 교환학생으로 와서 (   ) (I came as an exchange student and (   ).)

A.공부할 거야. B.공부했어. C.공부하고 있어 D.공부했지. E.공부하고 있었어.

394. A: 너는 생일이 언제야? (When is your birthday?)
　　 B: 나는 3월 11일에 (　　　　) (I was (　　) on 3/11.)

A.태어나지.　B.태어났어.　C.태어날거야.　D.태어났어?　E.태어나고 있다.

395. A: 크리스마스에 뭐할까? (What should we do on Christmas?)
　　 B: 가족과 함께 식사 (　　　　) (　　) meal with the family.)

A.했어.　B.했었지.　C.하려고.　D.하고 있지.　E.하고 있어.

396. A: 요즘 어떻게 지내고 있니? (How are you doing these days?)
　　 B: 열심히 아르바이트 하면서 (　　　　) (I've been (　　), working hard part time.)

A.살고 있어.　B.살았지.　C.살자.　D.살거야.　E.살겠어.

397. A: 내년이면 네가 몇 살이지? (How old are you next year?)
　　 B: 저는 23살이 (　　　　) (I (　　) 23 years old.)

A.되었다.　B.되고 있다.　C.됩니다.　D.되는 중입니다.　E.될 거야.

398. A: 학교에 언제 가니? (What time do you go to school?)
　　 B: 30분 후에 (　　　　) (I (　　) 30 minutes later.)

A.가고 있네.　B.가고 있어.　C.갈 거야　D.가는 중이야.　E.갔지.

399. A: 지금 어디쯤이야? (Whereabouts are you now?)
　　 B: 강남대로를 방금 전에 막 (　　　　) (I just (　　) gangnam-daero just now.)

A.지나고 있어.　B.지날 거야.　C.지났어.　D.지나는 중이야.　E.지나게 될거야.

400. A: 케이팝 콘서트가 언제지? (When is the K-pop concert?)
　　 B: 케이팝 콘서트는 이미 지난주에 (　　　　) (K-pop concert already (　　) last week.)

A.열릴 거야.　B.열렸지.　C.열릴까?　D.열릴 예정이야.　E.열린데.

Answer Key

371. D
372. C
373. A
374. A
375. D
376. A
377. B
378. D
379. D
380. A
381. E
382. A
383. E
384. A
385. B
386. C
387. D
388. A
389. D
390. C
391. C
392. D
393. C
394. B
395. C
396. A
397. C
398. C
399. A
400. B

VOCABULARY
단어공부

Select the correct word from the list and write it down.

우체부 목수 음악가 가수 경찰관 소방관

(Firefighter)

(Mailman)

(Police Officer)

(Carpenter)

(Musician)

(Singer)

과학자　　미용사　　기술자

의사　　이발사　　요리사

(Engineer)

(Scientist)

(Doctor)

(Hairdresser)

(Barber)

(Chef)

머리카락 | 이마 | 가르마 | 눈썹 | 귓볼 | 입술 | 눈

이 | 콧구멍 | 구레나룻 | 턱 | 코 | 보조개 | 귀

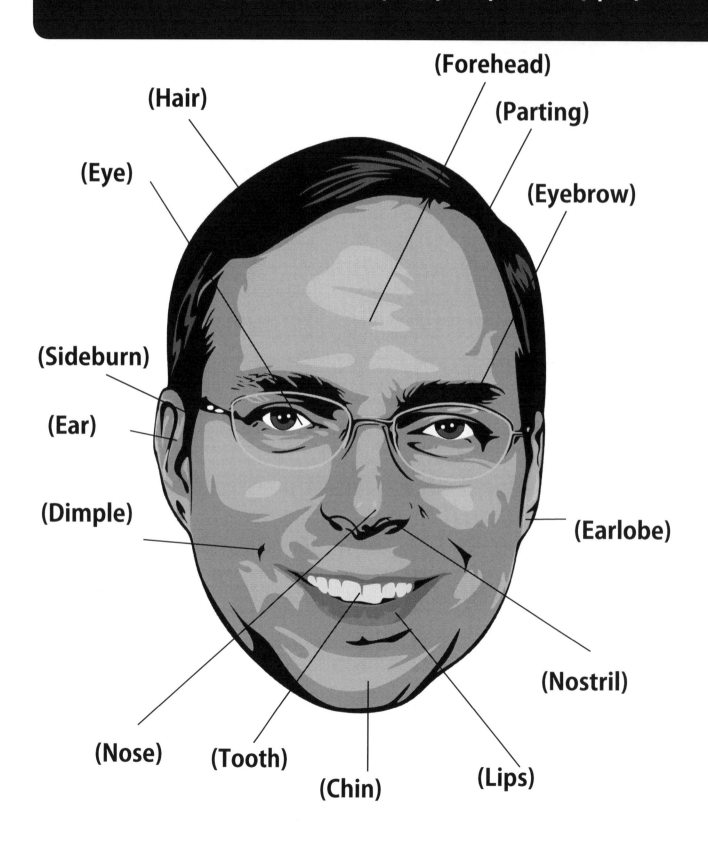

The following words are hidden in the scramble! Find and circle them.

gang ah ji : puppy   ji reum gil : shortcut

to yo il : Saturday   jeon hwa gi : telephone

gi reum : oil   adeul : son   won soong i : monkey

강 호 라 산 토 요 일 기 우 효
한 아 양 기 아 비 노 름 소 미
지 바 지 선 키 놈 종 큐 타 혜
름 키 송 전 화 기 구 미 코 아
길 아 들 구 리 원 긴 치 주 만
장 하 조 상 원 숭 이 양 풍 기

Ansewr Key

소방관 (Firefighter)

우체부(Mailman)

경찰관(Police Officer)

목수 (Carpenter)

음악가(Musician)

가수(Singer)

기술자(Engineer)

과학자 (Scientist)

의사(Doctor)

미용사 (Hairdresser)

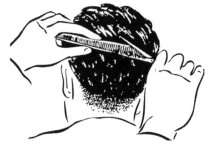

이발사 (Barber)

요리사 (Chef)

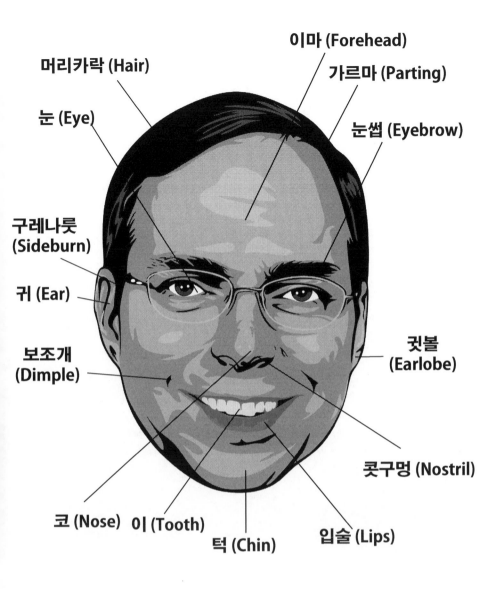

머리카락 (Hair)
이마 (Forehead)
가르마 (Parting)
눈 (Eye)
눈썹 (Eyebrow)
구레나룻 (Sideburn)
귀 (Ear)
귓볼 (Earlobe)
보조개 (Dimple)
콧구멍 (Nostril)
코 (Nose) 이 (Tooth)
턱 (Chin) 입술 (Lips)

강	호	라	산	토 요 일	기	우	효
한	아	양	기	아 비 노	름	소	미
지	바	지	선	키 놈 종	큐	타	혜
름	키	송	전	화 기 구	미	코	아
길	아	들	구	리 원 긴	치	주	만
장	하	조	상	원 숭 이	양	풍	기

SPELLING
철자법

Question 400 - 469. Circle the correct word that matches the definition.

401.

To Stop

막다 : 맑다

402.

How

어떷게 : 어떻게

403.

To Sit

앉다 : 않다

404.

To Reach

닷다 : 닿다

405.

What

무엇 : 무얼

406.

To Read

읽다 : 익다

407.

Yellow

노랗다 : 노랏다

408.

To Ripen

익다 : 있다

409.

To Cover

덮다 : 덥다

410.

Low

낮은 | 낳은

411.

Debt

빚 | 빗

412.

To Piggyback

없다 | 업다

413.

Correct

맞다 | 맏다

414.

To Forget

잊다 | 있다

415.

Ice

어른 | 얼음

416.

To Overturn

엎다 | 없다

417.

To Smell

맏다 | 맞다

418.

Light

빛 | 빗

419.

Dream

꿈 | 꿀

420.

To Connect

잇다 | 있다

421.

To Stack

쌓다 | 싸다

422.

Leaf

잎 : 입

423.

To Add

추가 : 추카

424.

To Close

닫다 : 닿다

425.

Locked Up

갇힌 : 가친

426.

Urgent

급한 : 그판

427.

To Subtract

빼다 : 배다

428.

Honest

정직한 : 정지칸

429.

To Open

열다 : 욜다

430.

Celebration

축하 : 추카

431.

Sunrise

해도지 : 해돋이

432.

Pretty

옙븐 : 예쁜

433.

Thoroughly

샅샅이 : 삿사치

434.

Fast
바른 : 빠른

438.

Day Time
낮 : 낮

442.

Thin
얇다 : 얕다

435.

Wide
넓다 : 높다

439.

Skinny
마른 : 무른

443.

To Fill
세우다 : 채우다

436.

To Find
찾다 : 찼다

440.

Knee
무릎 : 무릅

444.

Casserole
찌개 : 찌게

437.

Company
회사 : 홰사

441.

Sound
소리 : 서리

445.

Fish
물고기 : 물꼬기

446.

Chicken

닭 | 닥

447.

Sugar

설탕 | 솔탕

448.

Puppy

강아쥐 | 강아지

449.

Wall

벼 | 벽

450.

Cow

소 | 쇠

451.

Book

책 | 첵

452.

Kimbap

김밥 | 김빱

453.

Pillow

베게 | 배개

454.

Salt

속음 | 소금

455.

Rainbow

무지개 | 무지게

456.

Stair

계단 | 개단

457.

Library

도서간 | 도서관

105

458. Stomach

배 | 베

459. Crab

게 | 개

460. Butterfly

나비 | 납이

461. Desk

책상 | 책쌍

462. School

학교 | 하꾜

463. Grandmother

할머니 | 할먼이

464. Dragonfly

잠자리 | 잠잘이

465. Chair

의자 | 으자

466. Song

노래 | 노레

467. Snowman

눈사람 | 눈싸람

468. Turtle

거북이 | 고북이

469. Spoon

숟가락 | 숟가락

Question 470 - 500. Find and correct the misspelled words in the following sentences.

470. 땀을 많이 흘렸으니까 모곡을 해야겠다.
(I should take a bath as I sweated a lot.)

471. 아거가 큰 입을 벌리고 먹이를 먹고 있다.
(A crocodile is eating food with it's big mouth open.)

472. 하라버지께 어름물을 갖다 드렸다.
(I brought ice water to grandfather.)

473. 제 일음은 김철수입니다.
(My name is Kim Cheol-su.)

474. 노리터에 아이들이 많이 있구나.
(There are many kids at the playground.)

475. 책쌍에 앉아서 김빱을 먹었다.
(I had kimbap, sitting on a desk.)

476. 복도에서 뛰다가 너머졌다.
(I fell while running in the hallway.)

477. 버스 안에서는 손자비를 꼭 잡아요.
(Grab the handle tightly when in a bus.)

478. 강아쥐가 멍멍 짖습니다.
(A puppy is barking bow-wow.)

479. 와! 우리가 3:1로 승니했다!.
(Yay! We won 3:1!)

480. 동물의 반대말은 싱물이다.
(The opposite of animal is plant.)

481. 손가락에 반지를 꼈다.
(I put a ring on my finger.)

482. 도서간에 책이 참 만타.
(There are a lot of books in the library.)

483. 저의 꿈은 대통령이 되는 것 임니다.
(My dream is to become the President.)

484. 밥을 마니 머거서 배가 부르다.
(I'm full cause I ate a lot.)

485. 언니랑 옵빠랑 소풍 가야지.
(I should go on a picnic with my older sister and brother.)

486. 하늘에 구름이 하나도 없이 참 막다.
(The sky is very clear, without a single cloud.)

487. 운동을 열씨미 하면 건강에 조타.
(Working out hard is good for health.)

488. 비누로 손을 깨끄시 씻고 밥을 머거라.
(Wash your hands cleanly and eat.)

489. 뭐 잼있는 일 없을까?
(Isn't there anything fun?)

490. 학교에서는 선생님 말씀을 잘 드러라.
(Listen well to your teacher when in school.)

491. 피료하신게 있으시면 알려주세요.
(Please let me know if you need anything.)

492. 저녁 8시에서 10시 사이에 열락주세요.
(Please give me a call between 8 and 10 at night.)

493. 며칠동안 폭 쉬었더니 감기가 낳았다.
(My cold has gone away after I took a rest for a few days.)

494. 내일부터 일찍 이러나야지.
(I should wake up early starting tomorrow.)

495. 자리에 안자서 밥을 머겄다.
(I sat down on the seat and ate.)

496. 저는 여덜 살입니다.
(I'm eight years old.)

497. 다섯, 여섯, 일곱
(Five, six, seven.)

498. 동생이 귀찮게 해서 짜증이 났다.
(I got annoyed because my younger sibling bothered me.)

499. 지갑에 돈이 하나도 업다.
(There's no money in the wallet.)

500. 지갑을 일어버렸어요!
(I lost my wallet!)

Answer Key

401. 막다
402. 어떻게
403. 앉다
404. 닿다
405. 무엇
406. 읽다
407. 노랗다
408. 익다
409. 덮다
410. 낮은
411. 빗
412. 업다
413. 맞다
414. 잊다
415. 얼음
416. 엎다
417. 맡다
418. 빛
419. 꿈
420. 잇다
421. 쌓다
422. 잎
423. 추가
424. 닫다
425. 갇힌
426. 급한
427. 빼다
428. 정직한
429. 열다
430. 축하
431. 해돋이
432. 예쁜
433. 살살이
434. 빠른
435. 넓다
436. 찾다
437. 회사
438. 낫
439. 마른
440. 무릎
441. 소리
442. 얇다
443. 채우다
444. 찌개
445. 물고기
446. 닭
447. 설탕
448. 강아지
449. 벽
450. 소
451. 책
452. 김밥
453. 베개
454. 소금
455. 무지개

456. 계단
457. 도서관
458. 배
459. 게
460. 나비
461. 책상
462. 학교
463. 할머니
464. 잠자리
465. 의자
466. 노래
467. 눈사람
468. 거북이
469. 숟가락
470. 모콕 – 목욕
471. 아거 – 악어
472. 하라버지 – 할아버지 , 어름물 – 얼음물
473. 일음 – 이름
474. 노리터 – 놀이터
475. 책쌍 – 책상 , 김빱 – 김밥
476. 너머졌다 – 넘어졌다
477. 손자비 – 손잡이
478. 강아쥐 – 강아지
479. 승니 – 승리
480. 싱물 – 식물
481. 손까락– 손가락
482. 도서간 – 도서관 , 만타 – 많다
483. 임니다 – 입니다
484. 머거서 – 먹어서
485. 옵빠 – 오빠
486. 막다 – 맑다
487. 열씨미 – 열심히 , 조타 – 좋다
488. 깨끄시 – 깨끗이 , 머거라 – 먹어라
489. 잼있는 – 재밌는
490. 드러라 – 들어라
491. 피료 – 필요
492. 열락 – 연락
493. 낳았다 – 나았다
494. 이러나야지 – 일어나야지
495. 안자서 – 앉아서 , 머겄다 – 먹었다
496. 여덜 – 여덟
497. 일곰 – 일곱
498. 귀찬게 – 귀찮게
499. 엎다 – 없다
500. 일어버렸어요 – 잃어버렸어요

READING COMPREHENSION
(독해)

Question 501 - 510. Read the following passage and answer the questions.

●오늘은 규호의 생일입니다.

●규호는 열 살이 되었습니다.

●점심에는 학교에서 친구들과 햄버거를 먹었습니다.

●여동생 미나는 규호보다 네살이 어립니다.

●어머니께서는 규호에게 로보트 장난감을 선물 해 주셨습니다.

●미나는 카드를 선물로 주었습니다.

●저녁을 먹고 집에 와서 가족들과 함께 영화를 보았습니다.

●영화를 보고 강아지 맥스와 함께 놀다가 저녁 열한시에 잠을 잤습니다.

●참 행복한 하루였습니다.

501. Based on the passage, today is 규호's...

A.Birthday B.First Day at School C.Recital D.Mom's Birthday E.Dog's Birthday

502. Based on the passage, how old is 규호?

A.Four B.Nine C.Ten D.Eleven E.Twenty

503. Based on the passage, how old is 규호's sister, 미나?

A.Four   B.Six   C.Ten   D.Eleven   E.Twenty

504. Based on the passage, what did 규호 have for lunch?

A.Kimbap   B.Hamburger   C.Hot Dog   D.Noodle Soup   E.Pizza

505. Based on the passage, today is 규호 has a pet...

A.Dog   B.Cat   C.Iguana   D.Parrot   E.Hmaster

506. Based on the passage, what did 규호 get from his mom as a gift?

A.T-Shirt   B.Baseball Bat   C.Car   D.Robot Toy   E.Money

507. Based on the passage, what did 규호 do after dinner?

A.   B.Took a Nap   C.Played Video Game   D.Played Soccer   E.Watched a Movie

508. Based on the passage, what did 규호 get from his sister as a gift?

A.Card   B.Wallet   C.Ring   D.Shoes   E.Candy

509. Based on the passage, what time did 규호 go to bed?

A.Four   B.Six   C.Ten   D.Eleven   E.Midnight

510. Based on the passage, how does 규호 feel?

A.Angry   B.Happy   C.Rejected   D.Disappointed   E.Sad

Question 511 - 520. Read the following passage and answer the questions.

● 수미는 고등학교 2학년 입니다.
● 수미의 반에는 모두 오십이 명의 학생이 있습니다.
● 수미는 수학을 좋아합니다.
● 수미는 공부를 하는 것을 즐기지는 않습니다.
● 수미는 체육도 좋아합니다.
● 수미의 꿈은 수학 박사가 되는 것입니다.
● 학교에서 돌아오면 저녁 일곱 시가 됩니다.
● 가족과 함께 저녁을 먹습니다.
● 그 후에, 한강에 나가서 산책합니다.
● 집으로 돌아와 소설 책을 읽고 잠을 잡니다.

---

511. Based on the passage, 수미 is a(n)...

A.High School Student B.Middle School Student C.Artist D.Pianist E.House Wife

512. Based on the passage, which subject does 수미 like the most?

A.History B.Art C.English D.Chemistry E.Mathematics

513. Based on the passage, how many students are there in 수미's class?

A.Twelve B.Twenty C.Thirty-Two D.Forty-Five E.Fifty-Two

514. Based on the passage, does 수미 enjoy studying?

A.Yes B.No

515. Based on the passage, which subject besides mathematics does 수미 like?

A.Music B.Spanish C.Korean D.Chemistry E.P.E.

516. Based on the passage, what does 수미 want to be when she grows up?

A.Ph.D in Mathematics B.Engineer C.Computer Programmer D.Volley Ball Player E.Pianist

517. Based on the passage, what time does 수미 get back from school?

A.Four B.Five C.Seven D.Eight E.Nine

518. Based on the passage, who does 수미 have dinner with?

A.Father B.Friends C.Relatives D.Class Mates E.Family

519. Based on the passage, what does 수미 do after dinner?

A.Take a Stroll at the Han River B.Rest C.Sleep D.Practice Volleyball E.Watch a TV Drama

520. Based on the passage, what does 수미 do just before going to bed?

A.Drink Beer B.Read a Novel C.Surf the Internet D.Stretch E.Sing a Song

Answer Key

511.A   512.E   513.E   514.B   515.E   516.A   517.C   518.E   519.A   520.B

Question 521 - 530. Read the following passage and answer the questions.

● 시월 구일은 한글날입니다.

● 한글은 조선 시대의 임금인 세종대왕께서 만드셨습니다.

● 한글은 글자입니다.

● 한글이 만들어지기 전에는 중국의 한자를 사용했습니다.

● 한글은 매우 과학적인 글자이고, 배우기가 쉽습니다.

● 더욱 많은 사람이 한글을 공부할 것으로 예상합니다.

● 한글은 자음과 모음으로 구성되어 있습니다.

● 한글의 가장 큰 장점은 소리를 표현하는 글자라는 것입니다.

● 다른 언어의 발음 또한 자유롭게 표현할 수 있습니다.

---

521. Based on the passage, when is 한글날?

A.April 9th B.July 9th C.Every 9th Day of the Month D.October 9th E.December 9th

522. Based on the passage, who made 한글?

A.King Gojong B.King Joseon C.King Imgum D.King Sejong E.Queen Sejong

523. Based on the passage, 한글 is...

A.Letters B.Numbers C.Pronunciations D.Language E.Painting

524. Based on the passage, what were people using before 한글 was invented?

A.Japanese Characters B.Chinese Characters C.Latin Alphabet D.Mongolian Characters E.Hebrew Letters

525. Based on the passage, the author claims that 한글 is...

A.Scientific B.Romantic C.Complicated D.Unilateral E.Forbidden

526. Based on the passage, it is difficult for foreigners to learn 한글.

A.True B.False

527. Based on the passage, the author expects that less people will be studying 한글 due to its complexity.

A.True B.False

528. Based on the passage, 한글 is composed of...

A.Noun and Verbs B.Vowels and Consonants C.Numbers and Letters D.Nouns and Preciates E.Sounds and Pictures

529. Based on the passage, the biggest advantage of 한글 is that it expresses...

A.Sounds B.Meanings C.Symbols D.Ideas E.Emotions

530. Based on the passage, despite many advantages, 한글 is incapable of expressing the pronunciations of other languages.

A.True B.False

Question 531 - 540. Read the following passage and answer the questions.

●유산소 운동은 건강을 유지하는 데 있어서 매우 효과적인 방법입니다.
●전문가들은 일주일에 두 번 이상, 이십 분 이상 하는 것이
이상적이라고 말합니다.
●유산소 운동을 하면 심장 근육이 튼튼해지고 체지방이 줄어듭니다.
●따라서, 다이어트에도 큰 도움이 됩니다.
●하지만 무릎이 아픈 사람은 유산소 운동보다는
빨리 걷기가 더욱 좋습니다.
●규칙적인 유산소 운동과 함께 중요한 것은 균형 잡힌 식단입니다.
●유산소 운동 후에는 충분한 수분을 섭취하는 것이 중요합니다.

531. Based on the passage, what is introduced as an effective way to maintain health?

A.Boxing B.Cross Fit C.Yoga D.Cardio E.Weight Lifting

532. Based on the passage, experts say that it is ideal to run at least how many times a week?

A.Once B.Twice C.Three Times D.Four Times E.Five Times

533. Based on the passage, experts say that it is ideal to run for at least how long each time you work out?

A.Twenty Minutes B.Thirty Minutes C.Forty Minutes D.Fifty Minutes E.Sixty Minutes

534. Based on the passage, what is a benefit of doing cardio exercise?

A.Lose Body Fat B.Strengthens Knee Joints C.Improves Digestion D.Reduces Stress E.Improves Skin

535. Based on the passage, doing cardio strengthens which muscle?

A.Core B.Leg C.Arm D.Back E.Heart

536. Based on the passage, doing cardio exercise is beneficial for...

A.Dieting B.Studying C.Sleeping D.Focusing E.Resting

537. Based on the passage, who should NOT do cardio exercise?

A.People with Bad Knee B.People with Headache C.People with Heart Disease D.People with High Blood Pressure E.People with Diabetes

538. Based on the passage, what other exercise is suggested as an alternative for such people mentioned above?

A.Weight Lifting B.Yoga C.Pilates D.Walking Fast E.Rowing

539. Based on the passage, what else is equally important as doing cardio on a regular basis?

A.Well-Balanced Diet B.Low Body Fat C.Low Blood Pressure D.Resting E.Sleeping Well

540. Based on the passage, what is recommended after a cardio session?

A.Taking a Shower B.Taking a Bath C.Drinking Enough Water D.Sleeping E.Stretching

Answer Key

531.D   532.B   533.A   534.A   535.E   536.A   537.A   538.D   539.A   540.C

Question 541 - 550. Read the following passage and answer the questions.

> ● 동물에게 가장 힘든 계절은 겨울입니다.
> ● 추운 날씨에는 굶어 죽는 경우가 많습니다.
> ● 하지만 어떤 동물들은 한참 동안 먹이를 먹지 않아도 살 수 있습니다.
> ● 이러한 동물들은 겨울 동안 계속해서 잠을 잡니다.
> ● 이러한 것을 '겨울잠' 이라고 합니다.
> ● 예를들어, 북극곰은 계속해서 잠을 자면서
> 에너지 소모를 최소화할 수 있습니다.
> ● 봄이 오면, 잠에서 깬 북극곰은 다시 활발해집니다.
> ● 또 다른 동물은 개구리입니다.
> ● 개구리는 땅속에서 잠을 자면서 추운 겨울을 이겨냅니다.
> ● 과학자들은 이러한 습성이 진화의 증거라고 말합니다.

541. Based on the passage, the most difficult season for animals is...

A.Spring B.Summer C.Fall D.Winter

542. Based on the passage, during that time, animals often...

A.Freeze to Death   B.Starve to Death C.Kill Each Other D.Can't Mate E.Catch a Disease

543. Based on the passage, some animals can last through the winter time as they can live without having to...

A.Hunt B.Move C.Eat D.Mate E.Sleep

544. Based on the passage, what do such animals to during the winter time?

A.Save Energy B.Hunt C.Migrate D.Rest E.Sleep

545. Based on the passage, such behavior is called...?

A.잠 B.겨울 C.동물 D.날씨 E.겨울잠

546. Based on the passage, such behavior helps them last through the winter time as it...

A.Maximizes Metabolism   B.Minimizes Energy Use   C.Maximizes Fat Storage   D.Slows Down The Immune System   E.Slows Down The Digestive System

547. Based on the passage, when do the animals become active again?

A.Spring   B.Summer   C.Fall D.Winter E.Mid-Winter

548. Based on the passage, the author uses THIS animal as another example...

A.Tiger   B.Deer   C.Rattle Snake D.Fox E.Frog

549. Based on the passage, the above mentioned animal stays WHERE during the winter time?

A.Warm Region   B.Inside Another Animal C.Nest D.Cave E.Underground

550. Based on the passage, scientists say that such behavior is an evidence of...

A.Fight or Flight   B.Natural Selection C.Creation D.Evolution E.Revolution

Question 551 - 560. Read the following passage and answer the questions.

- 텔레비전을 너무 많이 보는 것은 눈 건강에 좋지 않다.
- 가장 큰 문제는 눈이 건조해지는 것이다.
- 심각해질 경우에는 시력을 잃을 수도 있다고 한다.
- 이러한 문제를 방지하기 위해서는 텔레비전을 한 번에 한 시간 이상 보지 말고, 눈을 충분히 쉬게 해 주는 것을 권장한다.
- 시력은 한번 잃게 되면 회복하기 쉽지 않다.
- 눈을 평소에 꾸준히 관리하는 노력이 필요하다.
- 이와 함께 눈 건강에 좋은 음식을 먹는 것이 도움이 된다고 한다.
- 당근, 블루베리에는 눈 건강에 좋은 영양소가 많아 자주 섭취하는 것이 권장된다.
- 그리고, 시력이 약해진 경우에는 안경을 쓰는 것이 필요하다.

551. Based on the passage, doing THIS too much is not good for eye health.

A.Reading B.Watching TV C.Exercising D.Sleeping E.Singing

552. Based on the passage, doing such can cause your eyes to become...

A.Dry B.Wet C.Stiff D.Malfunctioning E.Blurry

553. Based on the passage, such condition could lead to...

A.Loss of Hearing B.Stiff Eye Muscles C.Damaged Pupils D.Seeing Things E.Loss of Vision

554. Based on the passage, to prevent the problem, you should refrain from watching TV for more than THIS long at a time.

A.An Hour B.Two Hours C.Two Hours and Thirty Minutes D.Four Hours E.Six Hours

555. Based on the passage, giving THIS to your eyes is also important...

A.Time B.Pressure C.Light D.Rest E.Moisture

556. Based on the passage, lost vision can be easily restored with proper care.

A.True B.False

557. Based on the passage, how often do you have to take care of your eyes?

A.Frequently B.Once a Week C.Once a Year D.Consistently E.Sporadically

558. Based on the passage, doing THIS is also important for eye health.

A.Eating Food Beneficial for Eye Health   B.Sleeping More Than Six Hours a Day C.Taking a Walk at least Twice a Day D.Working Out Regularly E.Keeping Good Hygiene

559. Based on the passage, what are some of the good foods for eye health?

A.Ham Burger B.Rice C.Strawberry D.Blueberry E.Mushroom

560. Based on the passage, the author does NOT suggest wearing glasses in case of deteriorating vision.

A.True B.False

Answer Key

551.B   552.A   553.E   554.A   555.D   556.B   557.D   558.A   559.D   560.B

Question 561 - 570. Read the following passage and answer the questions.

● 운전할 때는 고도의 집중력이 요구된다.
● 특히나 날씨가 좋지 않은 날에는 더욱 조심해야 한다.
● 비가 많이 오거나 눈이 많이 오는 날에는 도로가 미끄럽다.
● 운전자가 조심하는 것이 가장 효과적인 방법이다.
● 전 세계적으로 하루평균 백 명 이상이 교통사고로 사망한다.
● 그중에서도 나이가 많은 운전자들이 일으키는 사고가 가장 많다.
● 이러한 이유에서 일부 국가에서는 팔십 세 이상 운전자들의
운전을 제한하는 계획을 하고 있다.
● 이러한 문제 때문에 많은 자동차 회사들은 자율주행 자동차를
개발하고 있다.
● 미래에는, 사람이 직접 운전하지 않아도 되는 시대가 올 것이다.
나아가, 전기로 움직이는 자동차가 대중화 될 것이다.

561. Based on the passage, high level of THIS is needed when driving.

A.Focus B.Understanding C.Analysis D.Humor E.Patience

562. Based on the passage, during THIS day the drivers have to be extra careful...

A.Bad Weather B.Holiday C.Weekend D.Hot Day E.Cold Day

563. Based on the passage, the reason it would be difficult to drive during a bad weather day is because the road is...

A.Congested B.Slippery C.Hot D.Uneven E.Damaged

564. Based on the passage, the author suggests which is the most effective way to avoid accidents?

A.New Technology B.Drivers Being More Careful C.Not Driving D.Renting a Car E.Car Pooling

565. Based on the passage, how many people on average die of car accidents?

A.Thirty B.Fifty C.Sixty D.Eighty E.One Hundred

566. Based on the passage, who are the biggest cause of accidents?

A.Teenagers B.Elderly People C.Unlicensed Drivers D.Female Drivers E.Male Drivers

567. Based on the passage, for the reason mentioned above, some countries are trying to restrict issuing license to the drivers over the age of...

A.Fifty B.Sixty C.Seventy D.Eighty E.Ninety

568. Based on the passage, for the reason mentioned above, many auto makers are making...

A.Self-Driving Vehicle B.Premium Vehicle C.Premium Vehicle D.Hydrogen Vehcile E.Robotic Vehicle

569. Based on the passage, WHO would be free from having to drive in the future?

A.Drunk Drivers B.Female Drivers C.Elderly People D.Everyone E.Teenagers

570. Based on the passage, WHAT would be a great help in protecting the environment?

A.Electric Vehicle B.Bicycle C.Smaller Vechile D.Hydrogen Vehicle E.Motorcycle

Question 571 - 580. Read the following passage and answer the questions.

● 한식은 한국인들이 즐겨 먹는 음식을 이르는 말이다.

● 한식의 역사는 수천 년에 달한다.

● 한식은 맛과 영양의 균형을 가장 중요하게 생각한다.

● 외국인들이 가장 좋아하는 대표적인 한식으로는 비빔밥이 있다.

● 비빔밥은 채소, 달걀, 버섯, 불고기 등을 함께 즐길 수 있는 요리다.

● 한식은 숟가락과 젓가락을 사용하여 즐긴다.

● 어른들과 함께 식사할 경우에는 어른이 먼저 식사를
시작하시기를 기다려야 한다.

● 한식은 이제 외국인들도 즐기는 세계적인 요리가 되었다.

● 한식의 미래를 위해서는 유행에 어울리는 새로운 레시피가 필요하다.

● 한식을 즐기는 젊은이들의 비율이 많이 줄어들고 있기 때문이다.

571. Based on the passage, the food that the Korean people enjoy are called...

A.Bap B.Hansik C.Achim D.Bibimbap E.Achim

572. Based on the passage, how long has its history been?

A.Ten Thousand Years B.Thousands of Years C.Thousand Years D.Five Hundred Years E.Hundred Years

573. Based on the passage, the most important aspect of Hansik is the balance between?

A.Yin and Yang B.Old and New C.Tradition and Trend D.Price and Quality E.Taste and Nutrition

574. Based on the passage, THIS Hansik dish is most enjoyed by foreigners.

A.Galbi   B.Kimbap   C.Japchae   D.Bulgogi   E.Bibimbap

575. Based on the passage, which of the following is not an ingredient of Bibimbap?

A.Mushroom   B.Egg   C.Bulgogi   D.Fish Cake   E.Vegetables

576. Based on the passage, Hansik is enjoyed using...?

A.Chopsticks Only   B.Spoon and Chopsticks   C.Hand   D.Fork and Chopsticks   E.Fork and Spoon

577. Based on the passage, when dining with older people, younger people must...

A.Not Talk   B.Wait Until The Older People Start Eating   C.Eat With Both Hands   D.Must Eat Less Than The Older People   E.Not Make Eye Contact With The Older People

578. Based on the passage, Hansik is now enjoyed by...?

A.Teenagers   B.Americans and Asians   C.Asians Only   D.Koreans Only   E.People Around The World

579. Based on the passage, what is needed for the future of Hansik?

A.Trendy Recipes   B.Traditional Recipes   C.Better Service   D.Healthier Dishes   E.Spicier Dishes

580. Based on the passage, the concern for Hansik today is that the number of people enjoying it is decreasing among...?

A.Koreans   B.Young People   C.Old People   D.Females   E.Males

Answer Key

571.B   572.B   573.E   574.E   575.D   576.B   577.B   578.E   579.A   580.B

Question 581 - 590. Read the following passage and answer the questions.

● 대한민국의 수도 서울의 역사는 오백 년이 넘습니다.

● 조선 시대에는 한양이라 불렸습니다.

● 서울에는 다섯 개의 왕궁이 있습니다.

● 서울의 인구는 약 천만 명입니다.

● 이는 도쿄와 뉴욕보다도 많은 숫자입니다.

● 서울에 사는 외국인의 숫자는 계속해서 증가하고 있습니다.

● 그래서 세계의 다양한 요리를 즐길 수 있는 식당들이 많습니다.

● 서울은 전통과 현대가 함께있는 도시입니다.

● 오랜 역사와 최신 기술이 자연스럽게 어울립니다.

● 하지만 차가 많아 교통이 복잡한 것은 단점입니다.

---

581. Based on the passage, how old is Seoul?

A.Over 100 Years   B.Over 200 Years C.Over 300 Years   D.Over 400 Years   E.Over 500 Years

582. Based on the passage, Seoul used to be called THIS during the Joseon Dynasty.

A.Saul   B.Sung   C.Gwanghwamun   D.Hyehwa   E.Hanyang

583. Based on the passage, how many royal palaces are there in Seoul?

A.Four   B.Five   C.Six   D.Seven   E.Ten

584. Based on the passage, the royal palaces are crowed with...

A.Soldiers B.Teenagers C.Students D.Tourists E.Historians

585. Based on the passage, Seoul has a population close to...

A.One Million B.Five Million C.Ten Million D.One Billion E.Five Billion

586. Based on the passage, Seoul has more people than Tokyo but less than New York.

A.True B.False

587. Based on the passage, the number of foreigners continue to...

A.Increase B.Decrease C.Stay The Same D.Stay at a Consistent Level E.Fluctuate

588. Based on the passage, there are many of THESE representing diverse cultures.

A.Schools B.Churches C.Restaurants D.Museums E.Theaters

589. Based on the passage, Seoul has THESE coexist in harmony.

A.Past and Future B.Men and Women C.North and South D.Tradition and Modernity E.Yin and Yang

590. Based on the passage, one downside of Seoul is...

A.Crime Rate B.Traffic Congestion C.Car Accidents D.Slow Internet E.High Living Cost

Question 591 - 600. Read the following passage and answer the questions.

● 언어를 공부하는 데 있어서 가장 효과적인 방법은 따라하기다.

● 어린 아기들이 언어를 배우는 과정을 보면 알 수 있다.

● 언어 학자들이 그러한 주장을 하고있다.

● 아기들은 부모가 말하는 것을 똑같이 흉내 내는 방법을 사용한다.

● 이러한 방법을 통해 의사소통하는 방법을 배운다.

● 이와 더불어 표정을 통해 감정을 전달하는 방법도 배운다.

● 어렸을 때 정확한 발음을 가르치는 것이 중요하다.

● 강아지들도 어미 강아지가 짖는 방식을 보고 따라 한다.

● 전 세계에는 약 육천구백개가 넘는 언어가 있다.

● 가장 많은 사람들이 사용하는 언어는 중국어다.

591. Based on the passage, the most effective way to learn a language is...?

A.Looking B.Listening C.Singing D.Writing E.Imitating

592. Based on the passage, a good example is...?

A.Teenagers B.Twins C.Teachers D.Old People E.Babies

593. Based on the passage, who makes such a claim?

A.Teachers B.Students C.Nurses D.Scientists E.Linguists

594. Based on the passage, whom do babies imitate?

A.Parents   B.Teachers   C.Nurses   D.Doctors   E.Friends

595. Based on the passage, through such practices, babies learn how to...

A.Balance Their Bodies   B.Walk   C.Communicate   D.Calculate   E.Sing

596. Based on the passage, what else do babies learn to use as a way of communication?

A.Facial Expressions   B.Fashion   C.Music   D.Color   E.Sound

597. Based on the passage, it is important to teach them THIS when they are young.

A.Correct Pronunciation   B.Gesture   C.Facial expression   D.Eye Contact   E.Listening Skills

598. Based on the passage, which animal learns to communicate through imitating their mom?

A.Bunnies   B.Iguanas   C.Puppies   D.Ducklings   E.Kittens

599. Based on the passage, how many languages are there in the world?

A.About Over 3,000   B.About Over 4,500   C.About Over 5,200   D.About Over 6,900   E.Exactly 6,900

600. Based on the passage, which is the most spoken language in the world?

A.Spanish   B.Portuguese   C.Chinese   D.English   E.Russian

For your Korean study needs,
check out our other titles!
at newampersand.com

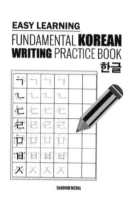

Let's Speak Korean (with Audio) - Learn Over 1,400+ Expressions Quickly and Easily With Pronunciation & Grammar Guide Marks - Just Listen, Repeat, and Learn!

Easy Learning Fundamental Korean Writing Practice Book - Learn And Improve Your Korean Alphabet Writing Skills

Fun & Easy Korean-English Picture Dictionary - Fastest Way To Learn Over 1,000+ Words and Expressions

The K-Pop Dictionary - 500 Essential Korean Slang Words and Phrases Every K-Pop, K-Drama, K-Movie Fan Should Know

The K-Pop Dictionary 2 - Learn To Understand What Your Favorite Korean Idols Are Saying On M/V, Drama, and TV Shows

How To Write a K-Pop Fan Mail / Letter in Korean - Complete Step-By-Step Guide With Over 400+ Expressions & Sample Letters

K-Pop BTS Quiz Book - 123 Fun Facts Trivia Questions About K-Pop's Hottest Band

K-Pop EXO Quiz Book - 123 Fun Facts Trivia Questions About K-Pop's Hottest Band

MERCHANDISE